Able-Bodied

Able-Bodied
scenes from a curious life

LESLIE SWARTZ

Published by Zebra Press
an imprint of Random House Struik (Pty) Ltd
Reg. No. 1966/003153/07
80 McKenzie Street, Cape Town, 8001
PO Box 1144, Cape Town, 8000 South Africa

www.zebrapress.co.za

First published 2010

1 3 5 7 9 10 8 6 4 2

Publication © Zebra Press 2010
Text © Leslie Swartz 2010

Cover photographs © Corbis/David H. Wells

'For Wilf and His House' © Leonard Cohen, in *Selected Poems* (New York: Viking, 1968)
'Prayer before Birth' © Louis MacNeice, in *Collected Poems* (London: Faber & Faber, 1966)
'At Seventeen', words and music by Janis Ian, © 1974, 1975 Mine Music Ltd/
EMI Music Publishing Japan Ltd
'Fuck the Disabled' © Greg Walloch, in Bob Guter and John R. Killacky (eds),
Queer Crips: Disabled Gay Men and Their Stories (New York: Haworth Press, 2003)

PUBLISHER: Marlene Fryer
MANAGING EDITOR: Robert Plummer
EDITOR: Lisa Compton
COVER AND TEXT DESIGNER: Monique Oberholzer
TYPESETTER: Monique van den Berg
PRODUCTION MANAGER: Valerie Kömmer

Set in 11.5 pt on 16.5 pt Adobe Garamond

Printed and bound by Pinetown Printers, Pinetown, KwaZulu-Natal

ISBN 978 1 77022 082 9

In (unreliable) memory of
Alfred Mervyn Swartz, 1921–1983

Contents

I

Homage and Violence

E very page of this book, every sentence, every word, is, in one
way or another, about my father. He died in 1983, when I was
a young man at the start of my professional life, neither of us
knowing how my life would turn out. Now I'm not much younger
than he was when he died, and I'm a bit amazed that I had no sense
then, when he died so suddenly, of how much I would miss him, or
of how, as I grow older, I want in some way to acknowledge him.

Another big surprise about growing older is that as the years
go by I see more of him in me. The little boy who was the image
of his mother is now in so many ways like his father – I see the
similarities in my face, my heavy thighs, my lumpy chest. But
my body is also different. Unlike my father, I do not have twisted
hammer toes and strange flat feet. I do not have the funny hip,
the blue mark below the skin on my side, the pronounced and
painful limp. And even though my own body is in some ways
like that of my father, I live on the other side of the divide: I am
able-bodied; he was disabled. Not that he would have wanted that
word, or the more trendy words (impairment, difficulty), said
about him or his body. But he lived – and my family and I lived

– with his difference and his pain, not spoken about much but always there.

Some years ago I went to a meeting at the Sandton Convention Centre at which people in the disability movement in South Africa were working on our contribution to the UN Convention on the Rights of Persons with Disabilities. I was new to the disability movement and to disability studies, and conspicuously white, male and able-bodied. But as I watched people moving around this large carpeted and mirrored space, in the gloom of half-light while we listened to speeches from the stage, I could see people walking around like members of my family – one limping heavily like my father, another walking with the same rolling gait as Auntie Tilly. I felt alone at the meeting, an anxious outsider, but somehow I also felt at home. I wept at the sense of having found a place of such familiarity to me and my family, and I felt guilty for weeping, as I sat there with all my white privilege and with my body in good working order – no pain, no difficulty getting around, nobody to point at me and laugh at my funny walking or talking.

My family was dominated not by my father's physical difficulties but by a group of women who were noisily organised around these difficulties and around their own. Chief among these was my paternal grandmother, forever angry about what she had done for her poor sick son, about how neither he nor anybody else seemed to care enough about how she had suffered and how much she had given up. Until my father's dying day, she berated him repeatedly and publicly for how he had made her suffer, from his miserable infancy ('I walked the floor with you!') to having to travel by boat to England with him for an operation, getting away just before the Second World War broke out, when he was eighteen. He broke her promise and her heart by refusing to become what she called a 'child specialist' – she never told us this, but I think she must have promised God that her Alfred would grow up to be a doctor and healer of children if only God spared his life, a life all the more precarious in the wake of the death of my father's elder sister before he was born. I know almost nothing about this phantom aunt, but she lives on in our family iconography as the 'monster'– physically very badly impaired, much more impaired than my father himself – who suffered and wrought suffering through a terrible, brutal infancy and then died very young. Whether my grandmother decided never to have children again after her second malformed baby was born I don't know, but I do have a sense of her bitterness at not only never having produced a 'normal' child, but also – after all she did, all her humiliation and pain – at my father's decision to become an engineer, to marry beneath him, not to give back what she deserved and what she had promised he'd give back.

But if my grandmother was large, loud, angry and bitter, she was not alone, and herein lies something of the mystery of disability in my family. Granny was the second-youngest of five children, four of them girls. (Poor Uncle Tubby committed suicide in the Belgian Congo before I was born – something about a business deal gone bad and Poor Uncle Tubby having been cheated out of his savings.) The youngest daughter was Auntie Leah ('But never, never call me that – I want to be known as "Lea"'), as painfully thin as Granny and Auntie Mary and Auntie Gertie (Gertie in particular) were fat. My mother's eldest sister, Auntie Tilly, who was close in age to my father's Auntie Leah, had first met Leah in the late 1940s, just as the world, and the Jewish world in particular, was trying to come to terms with what was being learnt about the Holocaust and the concentration camps. After this first and predictably unpleasant meeting, Auntie Tilly dubbed Auntie Leah 'the Buchenwald Chicken' (I'm not making this up) and the name stuck. While Granny had produced two deformed children, the Buchenwald Chicken had borne no children at all from her bony frame. By her own account, she had been blissfully happily married to Poor Uncle Jack, a vigorous, handsome and adoring husband. The family backstory on Poor Uncle Jack was that he supplemented his domestic bliss with women on the side, and had even kept a fancy woman in a bijou flat in Joubert Park. When I met the Buchenwald Chicken (or Auntie Lea, as I dutifully called her), she had recently been widowed, and we were all subjected to her misery and her loyalty to the memory of her dashing, but probably philandering, beau.

'Auntie Lea, wouldn't you like a hamburger?'

'No, my darling, Poor Uncle Jack loved hamburgers, so I won't eat them.'

'Auntie Lea, please come with us to see *The Sound of Music.*'

'How can you ask that when you know very well that Poor Uncle Jack loved musicals? You rogue!'

And so on. For many years, we had Granny living with us in what was then called Salisbury, Rhodesia, and at other times she and the Buchenwald Chicken would be with us for every weekend, requiring the house to be exorcised of all possible draughts and bad winds, and the curtains to be drawn at least partially, so neither sun nor wind should molest the delicacy of these elderly widows. Auntie Lea could never again live in Johannesburg and would have to stay in Salisbury, because she couldn't take the cold winters; she was just too delicate, and we all had to look after her.

Auntie Lea was also the great intellectual of her family. She and Granny had been born in South Africa of Latvian Jewish immigrants (the elder siblings were born in Latvia and came out as young children), and all the children had received very little education, apart from Auntie Lea, who had completed some years of high school. She even worked as a receptionist for her nephew who had a successful orthopaedic practice, an altogether more respectable calling than my father's own choice of working as an engineer at a dusty cement works. Being an intellectual type, Auntie Lea enjoyed a game of Scrabble, a game I too have always enjoyed. From about the age of eight I was able to beat her quite easily at Scrabble, but my instructions from my mother were always to let poor Auntie Lea win – which I mainly did. The half-joking but deadly serious complaining if she lost ('You scoundrel! You cheat! You little thief!') was just too much to bear. It was easier to let her crow about her superiority with words, which came, of course, from her love of Charles Dickens, and of Daniel Defoe's *Moll Flanders*, which, though it thrillingly chronicled the life of a prostitute, was old enough and classic enough to be a very respectable, and difficult, read.

Poor (but not Poor in the sense of Dead) Auntie Lea, then, could not eat hamburgers and could not go to movies. She could not take draughts, could not bear to lose, and was more delicate and clever than the rest of us put together. When we were old enough to speculate about it, my sister, Jenny, and I wondered whether a lot of this could not be put at the door of Lea probably never having had sex with Poor Uncle Jack, who clearly and sensibly had taken his pleasures elsewhere, but this does not matter here. On issues of debility and special attention, she won hands down against my altogether more substantial Granny, who had her own difficulties. Though Draughts and How to Avoid Them was high on Granny's priority list, this had nothing on her list of many allergies, which were protean and toxic to boot.

Granny had sensitive skin (this was true – I once saw her in the throes of an allergic rash and the red welts were not pretty) and she had been told by various doctors not to eat an ever-widening range of foods. This was not just a question of her not eating some things. It was the drama of her Not Eating Things that ruled our lives, as in:

'Oranges? I daren't touch them – much too acid – they give me allergies!'

'Tomatoes? Tomatoes? Who cooked with tomatoes – I daren't touch them! Where is that girl who cooked with tomatoes? I'll give her what for!'

'Lemon in the chicken? I can't take it! The irritation it will cause! You know I daren't!'

In this way, eating (of which she was very fond indeed) became at the same time an exciting, if potentially deadly, game of Russian roulette. One citrus fruit in the wrong place could lead to death or worse, or so we thought. Having inherited Granny's tendency to sensitivity (I get hay fever very badly), I am not unsympathetic to her allergies. But the drama of it all. Between inspecting foods for harbingers of destruction and trying to outwit noxious polar draughts which creep, as they will, into unsuspecting fifties-style houses in the subtropical climate of Salisbury, we had our hands pretty full. Add to this the poisons brought to (or taken away from) the table by the Buchenwald Chicken – no hamburgers or anything else that might recall the memory of Poor Uncle Jack – and it is hardly a wonder that all our meals, when Granny and the Chicken were present, were designed entirely around what they wanted and could eat. And in this there was no shame. My father, for example, loved the parson's nose when we had roast chicken, but there was never any question that when Auntie Lea was around, not only would she always be given the parson's nose, as she liked it too, but she would always use the opportunity to call my father a scoundrel for having even thought that perhaps this time he would get his turn to eat the tasty morsel. And none of this had any culinary or nutritional consistency either. After every meal, Auntie Lea's plate bore the detritus of what she could not eat. Thus, all chicken skin deemed 'too fatty' sat sadly on the plate alongside mielie kernels, and, on the very rare occasions we had them, piles of skins of grapes because the grape skins would ruin Auntie Lea's stomach and cause no end of trouble and tragedy. But the plate as battlefield after the dangerous business of eating Sunday lunch would never have as one of its casualties the parson's nose – far more fatty and greasy than any chicken skin. That, Auntie Lea could manage, and she was damned anyway if my father would have the satisfaction of getting the parson's nose, especially after what he had put his poor mother through when he was a baby, and now he wasn't even a paediatrician or married to an educated girl, either of which, we can only speculate, might have led to an arrangement of great pain to the Buchenwald Chicken, whereby she could have the parson's nose only every second Sunday and my father could enjoy it in between. An engineer with a common girl as his wife got only what he deserved.

In my family, then, getting older meant getting much more powerful, but it also meant (and this was the deal) getting more and more broken, because being broken was the ultimate source of power. And where was my father in this, my father with his really broken body, with his very real and ongoing severe pain, with his blue mark on the skin which opened and bled every winter, the result (I learnt only many years later, and I'm still not sure if the story is true) of his having been given a highly experimental – and toxic – radium treatment for his chronic projectile vomiting in infancy? In a word, he wasn't there at all. He was on the golf course.

My father loved golf with an irrational passion which I believe is not that uncommon among golfers. He was in so many ways a devoted father and husband – we got so much from him – but the weekend routine was well established. He would drive to pick up Granny and Auntie Lea from their dark flat in Rotten Row, bring them back to the house, and then, for all of Saturday afternoon and Sunday morning at least, he would be at golf. He would return from the golf course exhausted and often very sore, having limped around however many holes there were (there were no golf carts in those days, and even if there had been I don't think he would have used them), and having had a drink or two in the pub after the game, satisfied and happy in spite of the pain. I gather that he was a good sportsman, a person who overcame his impairments. (There is a family story of his having won a table-tennis competition on board the ship that was taking him to his major hip operation in London.) He would not countenance special treatment, he did not want to be different, and he loved his sport – golf in particular. At one stage my mother got him to play bowls, a game she enjoyed (though according to her she played very badly) and one which would make fewer physical demands on him. I remember seeing him hamming it up on the bowling green (he had a great sense of humour and was well liked), but his bowls career did not last long before he went back to golf and the long hours away from the world of difficult women – his mother and aunt. It was my mother's, my sister's and my job to look after that world, not that he wasn't treated to a barrage of demands from my grandmother as soon as he moved his aching body across the threshold of the house after his golf game. These demands ('Look at my income tax forms'; 'Contact that shyster lawyer who is trying to con me out of my small inheritance from your Poor Father'; 'Make me an appointment with the specialist for my skin') he met with a mixture of irritation, rage and resignation – he got irritable, even angry, all right, but my grandmother always got her way.

As I write, I worry about every word I put down, for a range of reasons. I worry that my (unreliable) stories about Granny and Auntie Lea will be seen as preposterous and made up, though at the same time I remember that my father's cousin's wife, similarly burdened by the disapproving and powerful fragility of the Aunties, as they were often known, began to call them 'Arsenic and Old Lace'. They are both long dead anyway, and though I remember my granny with a surprising warmth and affection, I don't much care if anyone thinks I am being unfairly harsh to the memory of the Buchenwald Chicken, about whom there was (in my memory at least) a spitefulness and a meanness, even a cruelty, which means that anything she gets in this or any other book will be her just deserts, hamburger or no hamburger.

But what about my father in all this – my father, with whom I had such a difficult and in many ways distant relationship, the father I pleased but mainly disappointed, the father I challenged and even, I think, humiliated? And what about the other two protagonists in this family drama, at this stage in my story still quite silent, both of whom are alive – my mother and my sister? I can easily anticipate what my mother, thoughtful and complex though she is as a person, would say about my belief that I disappointed my father: 'But your father was so proud of you. How could he not have been? Well, he didn't live to see all your achievements, but he would have been even more proud – you always did so well.' And so on. What will she have to say when she learns of my admission of my feelings of envy and even rage when I saw my father with his first grandchild – a grandson, Adam, now a wonderful adult and, as these things happen, a very successful academic in the field of psychology – radiating uncomplicated pride in this perfect little boy in his little stripy Babygro which my father labelled Adam's Parkhurst Rovers outfit? I knew I was being irrational and unfair, but I longed to get from my father what I thought he could give unconditionally to Adam but had not been able to give to me in our complex, competitive and sometimes rather cool father–son relationship. And what about my sister, who, though very dear to me, seems to inhabit a world so alien to mine, who claims to have no memory of parts of our childhood, who questions (as she should) at every turn my particular (paranoid?) take on things? For if this book is a love story, a tribute to my father, it is also a story of my getting my own back, stamping my version, my story, my take on things, with the authority of the printed word.

When my mother was a young girl, growing up the youngest child of six to poor Jewish immigrants in Johannesburg and Edenvale, she used words and writing in her own way to control her world, or so she says. My mother's youngest sister is almost ten years older than she is, and was known from the time she was very small as Baby, as she was for so long the youngest in the family (in her nineties she is still called Babe today). Babe had three older sisters and one much-adored brother. As my mother tells it, when her mother fell pregnant with her when Babe was nine, my grandfather would not speak to my grandmother. Eventually things thawed between the couple, and my grandfather said that he would be able to accept the child as long it was a boy, as he had so many daughters already. My mother was born and the rest, as they say, is history, a history of a choice to marry a man (and live very happily with him) who was seen by some as a cripple, not a real man, whose wife might, if he could have children, bear his crippled children, a man who would die young and leave my mother a young widow.

Well, my mother made her choice and it was, I think, a good choice. As it happens, both Jenny and I are able-bodied, but would it have been a bad choice if we had not been? I don't think so. But long before marrying my father, my mother was constructing the world for herself in her own way. She could write. She entered writing competitions in the newspaper and on the radio, and she won. On one occasion, my mother tells me, she was taken to meet another little Jewish girl who lived close to Johannesburg and who was also good at writing, a girl called Nadine Gordimer.

My mother wanted to be a journalist. She wrote to the *Sunday Express* asking for a cadetship, but was told that journalism was not a job for a girl. She went to Commercial High where, instead of focusing on literature and writing, she honed her skills at shorthand and typing (skills that remain excellent today). Her family was poor and she felt the burden of being the last child in the house long after her brother and sisters had moved off into their own lives, the only child of parents who did not get on very well – a father who had one failed business after another, and a mother who, though much loved by my own mother, had difficulties with her husband and did not speak to him at all for months before his sudden and unexpected death when my mother was seventeen. By this time my mother was long out of school. She had chosen to go to Commercial High in spite of her academic abilities, had skipped many standards lower down in school, tried to do the two years of matric in one year, and passed everything except Afrikaans by the end of the year. Instead of being a trainee journalist with matric behind her, she was, at the age of fifteen, finished with school but without a matric certificate. She became a shorthand typist, a very good one, but just a shorthand typist – a life certainly very different from that of Nadine Gordimer.

My mother is one of the most intelligent people I have ever met. She writes beautifully, and even in her eighties keeps up with and understands politics in a way few people do. Her life is a story of 'could have beens' – not that unusual for women of her age and background, to be sure, but this is her life. She would have made a wonderful journalist, historian or politician. My sister and I tried to convince her to go to university when we were teenagers (she would have got in as a mature student), but by then her confidence to do such a rule-breaking thing had ebbed away.

My mother could have written her own story of our family and she would have done it well. Had things been different, she could have captured our history (and her own) on the page, claimed the authority of the printed word. But she didn't, for a range of reasons, few of which I can pretend to understand. She had, I think, a very good life with my father, and is proud of her children and grandchildren. She had interesting if nominally lowly jobs – she worked in an office for most of her married life, partly for the money but also because she liked to work. She was always articulate and interested in things. I was very surprised when I found out as an adult that not all parents discussed the politics of the day every night around the dinner table. My parents were both part of the world, thinking about it, arguing about it, taking it on.

But not writing about it. I am the one writing about it, and about us. I have the confidence, the (inherited) ability to write things down, the education (paid for largely by my parents), the privilege of a job that pays me to write. I have the fancy laptop, the headphones with loud trashy music to keep me focused, the kitchen table to sit at, the libraries to visit and own. I have the track record, the PhD, the title of Professor. I am allowed, empowered – expected – to say things. And, boy, do I want to say them! I have all these things I want to say bursting out of me, threatening to cover every page, to blur and blot with their pro-fusion. I want to say these things because they mean something to me, about me. I want to do something to pay homage to my father and to where he (and his disability) have taken me, but I also want it to be my version, no compromises (well, not really – but compromises only on my terms). But in doing this, what am I doing to my mother's version, or even to my sister's version, of our lives? I know that as I write my mother and my sister into my story, I write their versions out, and in that way I do them violence. I can say it is all done out of love (and it is), but so much violence has been done out of love. I want to say sorry and I don't want to say sorry. I'm not doing anything wrong. But I am claiming something, privileging my take on the world, through this book.

I'm squirming as I write this and I am not altogether sure why. On one level, I'm embarrassed by 'Dear Reader' moments like this – I like narratives that sweep you along, stories that sing. But here's the rub: can my act of taking something for myself, doing this book, revelling in the writing, also be an act of giving at the same time? What gives me the right to dictate the terms of my gift, to call it a gift at all? The truth is, I can't separate any of these things out. I want and need to say something, but the minute I give myself that voice I am taking something away from the people I'm writing about. It is my memory I'll be relying on, a memory as unreliable as anyone else's. I will choose what to put in and what to leave out of my story. And in order to protect other people and myself, I will choose where to massage the facts deliberately, change names and places, tell lies. All of this in the service of the greater truth that I want to tell, a story which, though it starts with me and the vaudeville that is my family, has something more to say.

I'm not the first person doing what I'm doing – far from it. On the bestseller lists are endless accounts of people's miserable childhoods, stories of how they were beaten, bruised, locked up, ignored, set alight, misunderstood, overfed, underfed, over-indulged – in a word, spoilt rotten in all senses of that term. Some of these stories are really good, and I like reading them. But to what extent can we say that any of these is an individual story when so many of them adhere to the formula of the phoenix rising from the ashes, the triumph in spite of it all, the amazing power of the – so help me – human spirit? The truth is, since we're talking about truths, that we're all written into these stories as much as writing them or reading them ourselves. We over-come; we do well in spite of. There must be some literary theorist somewhere (there may be hundreds or thousands of them, for all I know) who has codified all the storylines that there are in literature and narrowed these down to just a few. In the case of today's popular life stories, we can have Triumph Over Adversity, or The Power of Forgiveness, or Miracles Do Come True.

So here I sit, with my father's memory palpably around me, with the silenced stories of my mother and my sister and who knows who else in the family threatening to pop up and make themselves heard if I do not keep them at bay, and with every cliché in the book ringing true when I think about my life and what I have to say, and I want to write a book about all this? Yes, I do. And I hope that in telling others I won't box them in too much, silence them, misrepresent them? Yes, I do. And at the end of all of this I want to come out smelling of roses (and not, as Granny would have it, 'Smelling of – excuse me – cat wee-wee')? Yes, I do. Well then, here goes.

2

A Social Story

I got into the world of disability studies as a research area quite late in my career, and almost by chance. Desperately out of place and unhappy at Stellenbosch University, where I'd been for a few months (hard for me to believe this, as I am so happy there now), I applied for and was given the opportunity to work for the new, revitalised Human Sciences Research Council (HSRC), on loan from the university for a three-year period.

When I joined the HSRC in 2002, it was a heady and very particular time. The HSRC had a history of collusion with, and of propping up, the apartheid government, and mixed in with some good social science work there was some shameful pseudoscience that was little more than veiled apartheid ideology. In the transition to democracy in South Africa, the HSRC had to change and to become a credible research organisation. With the charismatic, powerful and visionary Dr Mark Orkin at the helm, the 'new' HSRC was born, with a mission to do 'social science that makes a difference'. There was a bit of a frontier atmosphere in the HSRC at that time. The place was buzzing with new ideas, a new commitment to transformation in South Africa and (somewhat surprisingly to me, among others) a huge investment in turning what was a parastatal organisation into more of a business – getting money in and charging top dollar for research work.

I was quite overwhelmed by this business orientation and by the ruggedly male atmosphere of the HSRC ('Let's have another round of beers and *springbokkies* and let's *donder* this research proposal on the head'), an atmosphere to which powerful women in the organisation contributed as much as men. But I was also very excited to be there. It was a refreshing change from the backwater of academic life, and one of the myths the HSRC fast created for itself was that all the good research, the research that really mattered in the country, was being done by the HSRC itself. This was not true, but that did not stop me from feeling good about being on the inside.

In this pioneering spirit, I looked around the HSRC and found no formal focus on disability studies. I went to my boss at that time, Linda Richter, and pointed this out to her. Typically, and wonderfully, Linda's response was short, affirming and downright scary: 'Yes, you're right. You do it.' She was not interested in my protestations that I knew nothing about disability studies (which was true), or in my lack of confidence in my ability to do the job. 'We're all doing new things, making the place up as we go along,' she said. 'Of course you can do it.' That was that. Suddenly I was a disability studies expert. (Me and my big mouth.)

My first assignment as Mr Disability Studies – and in many ways the defining assignment of my working life – came to me out of the blue when I thought I was safe from such things. I was doing some work in the USA for a few months and was on leave from the HSRC for a bit. An email arrived from Linda, telling me that an HSRC colleague had successfully tendered for the work to develop an assessment tool to determine who should be eligible for disability grants. The client was the Department of Social Development, the branch of national government which dealt with all grants. In terms of having a chance to affect the lives of the poorest of the poor disabled people in South Africa, this was a big-time opportunity. Linda wanted me to head up the work on the grant, partly because I was a senior employee who did not yet have a major project to run and partly, I think, as a way of giving me a chance to establish disability studies as an HSRC focus, as I'd wanted to do.

But I didn't want it. I read through the successful proposal with a mixture of horror and fascination. A lot of it I didn't understand. Other parts I found very loose. I had a background in psychological assessment, and I just could not see how we would validly be able to assess the kinds of things we would be called on to assess. Too much was promised, I thought, much more than could be delivered, and the budget seemed to me to be hopelessly, fatally, unrealistic. It couldn't be done, and it couldn't be done even for double the amount of money we would have at our disposal. I emailed Linda that I wouldn't and couldn't take on the work, and that, anyway, it was rather unfair for me to be taking on a project that had been the brainchild of another colleague, who had put in all the work to win the tender. (I still feel guilty about taking over the project from this colleague and I don't think our relationship ever quite got over it.) Linda responded in her usual HSRC way: 'Nonsense. You are right for this job. You can do it and you will make a great success of it.' Case closed. I sat at my desk in a very snowy Boston and shivered from more than the cold.

Now I am sure you are expecting various kinds of story from here. How about something of *The Little Engine That Could* variety – we started from (worse than) nothing, we thought we could, we tried hard and in the end we delivered an amazing and triumphant disability assessment? Sorry. I'm not going to give you that kind of story, or even the end of the story (not now, anyway). But I will tell you something else.

As I read the successful proposal for the disability assessment work, I noticed (nobody could fail to notice) that repeatedly, and, to my mind at that stage, rather clumsily, the proposal promised that we would work in the 'social model' of disability rather than in the 'medical model'. I was not sure at the time what either of these models was, but I was savvy enough to know, in the same way that Two Legs Are Bad And Four Legs Good on the Animal Farm, that the medical model was going to be bad and the social model good.

The term 'medical model' echoed down the years for me. I had trained in psychology at the University of Cape Town (UCT) in the 1970s and 1980s, and had gone on to spend a happy few years in the psychology department there until I moved to Stellenbosch. I was an irritable and difficult psychology undergraduate – I far preferred studying English literature and mathematics, which were other subjects I took, but I wanted to be a psychologist. It seemed to me, and not just to me, that many of the lecturers we had in psychology at that time were rather more interested in dropping out, tripping out and tuning in than in being disciplined about their own work and teaching us. Nonetheless, it was a wildly entertaining time in many ways to be an undergraduate. Senior staff were to be seen under the influence both of Timothy Leary's philosophy and of the substances of which he was so fond. It was the era of kaftans, home-made sandals, holotropic breath work and, for one lucky graduate student of whom we were all quite jealous, lying conspicuously on top of your girlfriend on Freedom Square every lunch break. The psychology department, I heard, had been through a bad time just before I got there, with all sorts of nefarious practices. There were stories of white-coated scientists whose love life and scientific research had somehow got intermingled, as happens all too frequently in academic circles. Multitasking your sex life and your academic supervision, efficient but potentially abusive though this is, was in those pre-*Disgrace* days not really enough to get you into very big trouble. But the hotbed (so to speak) of scientific and sexual intrigue had been complicated, we were told, by a regime in which some staff were belittled and even spied upon. How much of this is a true or fair version of events I don't know and don't really much care, but what I do know is that by the time I got to the psychology department, the stirring words 'M—— for Prof!' were chalked on the wall in a revolutionary style appropriate to the times. M—— was at the time a very junior Young Turk academic who enjoyed the thrilling reputation of having taken on the mighty power of the White Coat, and all the abuse that went with it, and won. (Today M—— is a highly respected elder statesman in psychology, a pillar of the establishment, but that's another story.)

As undergraduates, we still did practicals using interesting bits of experimental apparatus, and learnt about the Split Brain in Man (this was before feminism – women have a Split Brain too). We even heard about chimpanzees and pigeons and rats being experimented on in the department, though I never saw a chimp or a pigeon or a rat, much as I would have liked to have seen one pressing a lever or pecking at a disk, all in the name of food (from the animal's point of view) or in the name of science (from ours). But the writing was on the wall, literally ('O—— for Prof!'), for science and white coats in our department. In came Unconditional Positive Regard and Empathy, out went neuropsychology (though we did have some lectures showing how if you fill a bucket with gelatine and shake it about you get perfect EEG waves); in came Rolfing and Body Work, and out, in its right-wing, Western, anti-democratic physiological sense, went the body as object of study. There were two enemies: scientists in white coats, and their even more powerful evil cousins, medical doctors.

What a time it was for social science and our understanding of people. In 1960 Thomas Szasz had published *The Myth of Mental Illness*, arguing that what he termed 'problems in living' were not reducible to physical, neurochemical processes, and that it was incorrect (and politically reactionary) to try to explain conflict between people, and issues of power and struggle, in terms of what was happening in people's heads. It's hard to believe in these super-neurological times, when everything under the sun is a brain disorder, that Szasz's ideas had much purchase, but they resonated with the mood of the time, with talk about social conflict and social action, with the desire to overthrow old authorities. Given that in South Africa the 1960s got going only in the 1970s and 1980s, Szasz was all the rage during my undergraduate and most of my graduate years. 'Mental illness' was not an illness at all – it was all social, interpersonal, intergroup, and not at all medical. R.D. Laing, a Scottish psychiatrist, had become a cult figure for his work claiming that madness (he too did not like the term

22

'mental illness') was caused by disturbed relationships and toxic families. Like many other psychology students in Cape Town in the 1970s, I owned well-thumbed copies of his books, including *Sanity, Madness and the Family*, published by Laing and his co-author Aaron Esterson in 1964. This book contained gripping case studies of families apparently determined to destroy the lives of their children.

In 1971, the left-wing filmmaker Ken Loach made a Laingian film called *Family Life*. It told the story of a young woman with schizophrenia made mad by her parents and showed, with breath-taking drama, scenes of the parents doing exactly what Laing (and other family theorists of schizophrenia at the time) had described. I recall a scene in which the parents of this hapless woman nodded and gestured to each other about her in her presence, and then expressed amazement that she felt any discomfort at all – her valid reaction to their abuse was seen as evidence of her illness. I must have seen *Family Life* at least three times at the Labia Theatre in Orange Street, just reopened as a cinema from the crumbling ruins of a failed live theatre, and a cheap place where students could go to see classic and art films. In our group, one of the worst things we said about a fellow student was that she 'didn't like *Family Life*'. It is hardly surprising that the message of *Family Life* and of the whole Laingian enterprise – which was essentially 'They fuck you up, your mum and dad', as poet Philip Larkin put it – appealed so completely to us as angry adolescents in a country blighted by a right-wing and racist government. Today both Laing and Szasz are, with good reason, regarded as classical thinkers in the history of psychiatry, and they taught us a great deal. But when I think of the damage these so-called progressive thinkers (and a progressive filmmaker like Loach) did to the lives of people and families dealing with the real live challenges of severe mental illness (a term I no longer apologise for using), I become very angry.

It was not just the left wing of psychiatry that was in on the act. Bruno Bettelheim, much loved still for his psychoanalytic work on fairy tales, was also responsible for popularising the term 'refrigerator mothers' to describe the mothers of children with autism. I don't think there is anyone around today who has any doubt at all that there is a medical basis for autism, but in those thrilling days, when society and its most oppressive institution, the family, were seen as the root of all evil, comparing a parent of an autistic child to a Nazi concentration camp guard (as did Bettelheim, himself a concentration camp survivor) seemed like a progressive and humane thing to do.[1]

The medical model, then, along with the white coat of the laboratory scientist, was bad news, and we believed fervently that everything – every human problem – could be attributed to society and its oppressions. We were right, of course, about the importance of social factors and of oppression. These affect how any person anywhere lives with any difficulty, including difficulties of clearly organic origin. But our view was total: the medical model was wrong. Some of our fervour came from being in the South Africa of the late 1970s and early 1980s – a South Africa after the 1976 uprisings but with no sense, no hope, that the apartheid state would be dismantled in our lifetime. And there was no doubt at all that apartheid caused misery, and indeed madness, on a grand scale. Perhaps also because of the politics of the time we policed our own views and those of our colleagues and friends quite zealously. When I was doing my first year of professional training in clinical psychology, we were taught by an eccentric and gifted psychiatrist who was especially interested in organic psychiatry and brain pathology. Much to my own surprise, I too became intrigued with organic psychiatry and with the many ways in which physical factors, including infections, trauma and nutritional deficiencies, can lead to symptoms that mimic those of what in those days we termed non-organic, or 'functional', psychiatric disorders. I found it fascinating (and important for my future work as a psychologist) that, for example, a person with thyroid problems may appear to have an anxiety disorder, a disorder that disappears when the thyroid problems are properly treated. For this sudden interest of mine in the so-called medical model I was brought sharply into line by one of my fellow trainees, an earnest but unimaginative person who told me that it was part of my role as a psychologist to 'take a stand'. When I told her that in fact I had taken a stand – a stand in which I thought organic psychiatry was important – she made it clear that there was only one stand a respectable psychologist could take, and that was a stand against the white-coated enemy and the hated 'medical model'.

I have to say that I was convinced, and remain convinced, by some of the argument against the medical model in psychiatry. It is a problem, and a serious one, that difficulties among people, some of which result from the abuse of power, may be reduced to medicalised categories. I was once at a psychiatric meeting in New York attended by Robert Spitzer, who was responsible for the development of a radical new psychiatric diagnostic system. Published in 1980 as the *Diagnostic and Statistical Manual of Mental Disorders*, third edition (DSM-III), Spitzer's work is essentially a process of systematising contemporary psychiatric diagnosis in the USA and, to a great extent, worldwide. Another delegate expressed his concern about how many aspects of contemporary life, and difficulties in relationships among people, were now being called medical 'syndromes'. He said, 'Soon you will have a new diagnosis called "Joking Disorder" for people who tell too many jokes.' I don't remember Spitzer's response, but I thought his interlocutor had a point. On the other hand, it would only be a wilfully obtuse person who today could ignore the remarkable and exciting progress made in our understanding of the relationship between the brain and behaviour. I have many regrets that all I learnt of neuropsychology at university was about shaking tubs of gelatine and getting EEG waves, and I feel that one of the most exciting areas of contemporary study has passed this old man by.

When I saw the proposal in 2002 for our HSRC work on disability grants, then, with its repeated references to the 'good' social model and the 'bad' medical model, among my first reactions was, 'This is So Last Century. I (and we) have done enough trashing of the medical model in psychiatry and psychology to last a lifetime.' Well, things are a little (if not very) different in disability studies, and I was to learn that this social/medical model divide would become central to almost all my work after 2002, Last Century or not. When I got back to South Africa in early 2003 and shakily and reluctantly took on the role of principal investigator in our study, one of the first things I had to do was to attend a meeting to present our work plan to representatives of the disability movement. The first concern expressed by these representatives was that, because many of the people on our team were health professionals, it was not likely that we were sincere in wishing to work in the social model. They seemed to imply that just as their backs were turned we would pop the medical model back in again. I came to learn over time that the disability movement in South Africa and elsewhere has a long history of being duped by researchers – people who promise a lot and deliver little or nothing, and who are not really sincere about the issue of disabled people's rights. The representatives were right, therefore, to be suspicious, but for me it was a bit of a shock to be painted so clearly as the 'other'. I had the good sense and political savvy to emphasise our commitment to the 'social model', and by the end of the project the suspicions between us had, as far as I am aware, evaporated, but I still didn't really understand what this focus on the 'social model' meant. I'm not sure I do fully understand it even now, but I think it's important, and certainly not as simple as it seems.

The essence of the 'social model' as put forward by disability activists in Britain in the 1970s was that the key to disablement lay not in whatever impairment a person may have, but in the social conditions which oppress people with impairments, and the barriers that there are in society which restrict full participation by disabled people.[2] If, for example, a wheelchair user wants to work for a business which is located on the upper floor of a building without a lift, it is not really the wheelchair user that's the problem – it's the fact that the building is not accessible. Similarly, when it is said that a person who has a facial disfigurement cannot work as a receptionist because he or she will 'upset' the public, there is something going on here which is not about the disfigurement at all; it is about excluding someone from work because of prejudice against people with facial disfigurements. In the social model, then, the impairment – the physical characteristic, health condition or feature that makes the person to be seen as different from others – is not sufficient for disablement to occur. What disables people – what makes people disabled – is how society responds to the impairments. In the British social model, then, we call people 'disabled' because they are, as the model puts it, 'disabled by society'. The Americans tend to prefer the term 'people with disabilities', as they argue that the disability should not be seen to define a whole person. I won't now go into all the infighting about exactly which words are right to use. It's easy to see, though, how important it was for the disability movement to establish the centrality of oppression and the abuse of power to understanding disability. Equally important was taking the authority for disability away from medical 'experts' who focused on impairments and giving it to disabled people themselves – the only people to know from the inside what it is like to be disabled.

According to the social model, then, was my father disabled? (As I write this, I once again sense him squirming at this discussion – he would never have called himself disabled.) He certainly had impairments and he lived with pain. He had, in the words of the song in *My Fair Lady*, a 'large Wagnerian mother', some of whose largeness (fat but not tall, she seemed huge) and anger were about her sense of having had more than her share of burdens, including my father with his physical problems. But gathering from the unique charms of the Buchenwald Chicken, Granny would probably have been loud and Wagnerian anyway. My father went to a good school, got a university education, did the course he wanted to, and spent quite a lot of time limping around geological sites and cement factories as he worked in the cement business. Was he excluded from full participation in society? I don't really think so. But he also made sure he wouldn't be. Not everybody with his impairments would have chosen to limp around golf courses, for example, but he loved his sport, and being a sportsman was part of his identity. He had operations until late in his life (the last being, literally, to fillet his toes – he showed the bill around proudly, along with a vigorous display of his now boneless and therefore floppy four toes on his left foot!). He had a career, and was successful at it. He worked for a large, British-based multinational company, which for most of the time he was there was quite a conservative organisation. When he became entitled to a company car, he was forced to drive a tank-like Wolseley, a quintessentially old-fashioned car with high Tory written all over it. He hated it, but that's another story.

In the years immediately before my father's death, a new corporate culture descended on his company. Out went the old style of genteel (if secretly cut-throat) Britishness, and in came a younger, robust, more flashy, American corporate style. Out with white shirts with the business suits, in with bright pink and purple shirts. Out with golf as a compulsory part of doing business, in with squash and saunas. Lots of drinks after work became the order of the day. My father hated the drinks rituals but he reluctantly participated, and would sometimes come home a bit the worse for wear and in a foul temper. But with his impairments he could not play squash. And, with his beautiful white hair (which had gone white in his thirties) and wrinkled skin (wrinkled from too much sun on golf courses but also from years of working at cement factories), my father looked, and seemed, old. He was courtly towards women (whom he always respected) and, unlike more than one of his colleagues, he was not having an affair with his secretary. He began to find that business decisions were taken in places where he was not – in the sauna at the squash courts, at expensive dinners to which he was not invited but about which, he suspected, some secretaries knew more than he did. He was slowly eased out of things, or felt that he was, and when he took early retirement (with a very generous settlement from the company) it was with great relief on both sides. He no longer fitted the profile, and his kind, old-fashioned good manners were now surplus to requirements. Within a few months of retiring, he was dead of a sudden heart attack.

I have strong feelings about my father's company, the place he never quite fitted in, but for which he worked very hard and for very long hours for almost thirty years. I don't have a shred of evidence for this, and I am almost certainly being unfair and irrational, but I hold that company and some of the people who worked for it responsible for my father's early death. I watched him being humiliated and excluded, all of which he handled with dignity. When a kindly relative said of my father at the funeral, 'He was such a happy person,' I wanted to hit him. My father was many things – generous, humorous, kind, respectful – but to call this complex and difficult man, who had been slowly brutalised by corporate renewal, 'happy' seemed to me to miss the whole point of the man, to belittle him, to refuse to see him. Something had been done to my father and he had stood up to it with all the strength that he had. He had done so ever since he was very small and a source of dreadful, deathly anxiety to his own parents, as well as being a source of shame. On his own terms he had triumphed – he had the career he wanted, played the sport he loved, loved and married the woman he chose – but for me something horrible happened towards the end, a full circle in which suddenly his broken body and his filleted toes came again to mean something more than just impairments. This, for me, is the social model.

There are hundreds, thousands, probably millions of stories similar to this story, which is my story of my father. And not all of them are about disability either. How many women have been excluded from things because they did not play golf with the boys and drink in the pub? How many black people have been seen as unequal to a range of tasks because of their skin colour? How many gay people? How many Muslims? How many Jews? My father's Jewishness, another way in which he did not fit his Anglo-Christian workplace, is another part, an important one, of his story. None of this diminishes the point about the social model; in fact it strengthens it. What disability theorists in the tumult of the 1970s made clear is that disablist oppression is not separate from other forms of oppression, nor is it qualitatively different. Disablism is, if you like, a racism against disabled people, a patriarchy of a kind. And given that all our identities are complex and layered, being disabled may be only one part of things. And having an impairment confers no necessary nobility or understanding of the oppression of others. When I was at university in the 1970s, I was friendly with the only woman student in the engineering faculty; she was doing the same degree that my father had done many years before. A male friend of mine said that he supposed when she qualified she could go into the cosmetics industry, as this was the only place where he could imagine a female engineer working. When I told my father this story, he said, true to form, that he saw no reason why she could not work in the cement business or any other 'manly' business. But had she come to work with him in the 1970s, would he have stopped having business conversations on the golf course and at the nineteenth hole? I doubt it.

It's easy for us to claim that we don't discriminate against people, but it's much harder to live up to the claim, and I include myself in this. But I want to tell another social-model story, one with a happier ending. I had not been an academic for very long when I met Brian Watermeyer, whose research work I supervised in his honours year at UCT. Brian was a very bright and articulate student, and we got on well. He has retinitis pigmentosa, a chronic and deteriorating condition, and by the time he got into the honours programme his visual impairment was substantial; in fact he was legally blind. (His elder brother, Michael, a lawyer who worked in the Disability Unit at the university, was completely blind and used a cane and a guide dog.) One day Brian came to me in some distress. He wanted to apply for a master's degree in clinical psychology, a much sought-after degree in South Africa as in many other parts of the world, and he had just been told by the director of the programme that he could not be considered, because he was blind. Before starting as an undergraduate, Brian had come, together with his parents, to see the head of our department (who was not a clinical psychologist) to ask if clinical psychology would be open to blind trainees. The departmental head had assured him that we would train blind clinical psychologists if they met the selection criteria. Having completed his three undergraduate years and now in his first graduate year, Brian was told that this was not so. He was devastated by this decision.

I talked with my colleagues about this situation, and it was clear that I was by no means the only staff member who felt angry that the director of clinical psychology training had made an ex cathedra statement to Brian without consulting with us and without, it seemed to me, thinking through what this meant for Brian or for the department. But I have to say that this mistake by a colleague opened a door, and a world, to me. Colleagues and I began to work quite hard to explore the issues involved in training blind psychologists, and I took to it with a fervour fuelled by my own particular past. We contacted universities worldwide about how to train blind clinical psychologists (it did not take us long to find out that many had been successfully trained, nor were we surprised at this), and I became proficient at a new thing called electronic mail, or email. This entailed going to the university computer centre and typing messages on the single terminal devoted to this purpose in the entire university, booking time on the terminal for the next day and hoping against hope that people would reply. I also had some meetings with Brian, Michael, and Kate Jagoe, who had established the Disability Unit at UCT. Kate had a spinal cord injury and was a wheelchair user. She was an artist by training, and all over her office were sketches of beautiful (and able) bodies by a range of artists. I did not miss the political point about the rights of disabled people to enjoy, as we all do, looking at beauty. Kate taught me a lot: she was accommodating and pragmatic, and did not blame me for my woeful ignorance of disability issues. Instead, she taught me. I learnt about patience and indefatigability, about being prepared to listen but not allowing oneself to be bullied, and about keeping at the centre of everything disabled people's right to the same benefits and responsibilities as others.

Through the sudden illness of my colleague (and somewhat to my alarm but, in retrospect, great luck), in the midst of all of this I became director of our clinical psychology training programme. It became my job, now, to work with colleagues on the issue of whether we would be prepared to train blind people as clinical psychologists. We were determined to keep the issue of principle separate from the particular case of Brian, and it was important not to conflate the person with the issue. On the whole there was a lot of support for opening up our training to blind people, but there were three areas of concern. One involved questions about inherent parts of the job – how, for example, could a blind person do a neuropsychological assessment which involved assessing how a patient copies a drawing? As it turned out, this issue could be dealt with quite easily. Provided a blind psychologist has an assistant who can see and who can administer tests on the psychologist's instructions and carefully and accurately describe what has been drawn, the blind psychologist, using knowledge from the neuropsychology literature, can make an informed assessment. There are many other ingenious methods which have been used, including tactile ones (one psychologist in the USA learnt to 'read' drawings by having raised imprints of these made, which were then pressed against the skin of the psychologist's back), but it was clear it could be done.

The second argument that some colleagues made against allowing a blind person to train as a psychologist was that psychologists use visual cues to assess people; we 'read body language'. This is true, but I didn't know then, and still don't know today, of any research that assesses how important visual cues are to the work of a psychologist. Even if this research exists (and it probably does), the more important question is whether there are ways in which other cues (apart from the visual ones) can be used to form a meaningful clinical impression. When I heard the arguments about 'visual cues', I replied with the truism that blind people may develop better ways of reading cues through sound, through the ways in which people speak and don't speak. There could, of course, be serious difficulties in cases where people are completely mute, but this occurs quite rarely, and people who are mute pose challenges to sighted psychologists too. At the time I did not think of this, but there was also something problematic implicit in what my colleagues were saying. Did they believe that blind people in general were less able to pick up subtleties about human interaction than are sighted people? And how much of the concerns that some colleagues had about 'body language' could be put at the door of professional competence and how much attributed to the way in which psychologists think about their own professional culture? Was it hard for colleagues to imagine a blind psychologist in the same way that in the 1970s we had trouble imagining a female engineer?

Some of the answer to this question was provided, I think, by the third set of objections raised by colleagues. People who worked with dangerous patients were worried about the safety of a blind psychologist among such people. The solution to this – though this is easier said than done in hospitals with a serious lack of funding – is to make sure that there is adequate security. This kind of objection merged into a further objection: that during training, psychologists have to work at a number of hospitals and therefore have to be able to drive between hospitals. This is patently nonsense, and people who can't drive can be accommodated quite easily, but once again it shows how our social or cultural beliefs about what a profession or activity is are constructed around those who have historically had access to that profession or activity, and that we come to see this profile as what is required. We then blame the impairment and not the way we organise our society for the barrier.

What was absolutely clear to me in Brian's case was that the visual impairment was in fact far less of a problem to our training him (or other blind people) than the way parts of our profession, as representatives of a disablist society, closed ranks in the face of difference. The end of the story, though, is a good one. The more we thought as a group about the issues (and Kate Jagoe helped us a lot with this), the more it became clear that we could and would train blind clinical psychologists. Brian was eventually trained, was top of his class, and is now a colleague and friend, and an important contributor to the psychoanalytic literature on disability.

I think in the end that we did quite well by Brian, but the same can't be said for every university to which he applied. The worst story is about a university in South Africa that prides itself on being a liberal and inclusive institution. Brian made it clear on his application form that he had a visual impairment, and he was delighted to be shortlisted for a place on that university's training course. Invited for an interview, he paid a large sum of money (as do other candidates) out of his own pocket to fly to the university, which was in another part of the country. Once there, he was doing very well in the process by which the shortlist is winnowed down. All was going well until he was called aside by a senior staff member who said, 'Brian, I'm sorry, but we don't have the resources to train a blind person. We will not be able to offer you a place.' Brian was sent home.

I still get angry when I think about this story. The university had allowed Brian to fork out money and to go through all the stress of selection, and had then told him they were excluding him on the basis of an impairment which they knew he had before he came to be interviewed. They offered no compensation to him. Now it could be that in fact they did not like Brian for other reasons and simply used the impairment as an excuse. If this were so, such an approach, apart from being dishonest and pusillanimous, would be deeply disablist, and would show an even worse understanding of the politics and personal experience of disability. It could also be that Brian was mistaken or lying about what had happened, but knowing Brian I did not believe this for a minute.

Some years later I got a call out of the blue from a young man I knew who had a visual impairment. He needed advice. 'You see,' he said, 'I've just been shortlisted at [the same university at which Brian had been shortlisted]. I got through all the individual and group interviews, but just towards the end I was taken aside by one of their profs, who told me they couldn't train me because I'm going blind. I flew all that way and spent all that money for nothing.' I advised him to contact Brian (now a qualified clinical psychologist) and to lay a complaint. I felt ashamed that I had not imagined all those years ago that the university would not of itself have learnt some lessons from what it had chosen to do to Brian.

Years later, I heard about the golfer Casey Martin in the USA. Martin had a circulatory disorder in his leg and became unable to walk between holes on the golf course. There were huge objections to his being allowed to use a golf cart on the professional PGA Tour. One objection I heard was that his using a cart would remove 'athleticism' from the game. Another objection was that his using a cart would affect the 'culture' of the game – golf, after all, is 'about' walking around a course. I'm not a sports expert or a physiologist, but when I hear such objections I hear the echoes of people saying, 'We can't have women around here because it would affect the culture of our work/sport.' Or, we can't have black people. Or (since we are talking about golf) we can't have Jews. My father was excluded from many golf clubs on the basis of his being Jewish, and black people were also kept out (including by clubs that would admit my father).

The point of the social model, for all its difficulties, is that it forces us to look at discrimination for what it is. And things pop up to trip you. Shortly after arriving at the psychology department at Stellenbosch, I met a blind psychologist who had been trained in that department with minimal fuss and bother. I was keen to work with him and invited him to lunch. The afternoon began badly, with an extremely embarrassing and frustrating perambulation through the town in which I as a newcomer with a dreadful sense of direction tried (for a long time unsuccessfully) to find out from a blind person the location of a restaurant where we were to have a working lunch together. But once we were settled, we got chatting easily and things got much better. I commented that I was so pleased that he had been trained with so little trouble and fuss at Stellenbosch. He was also pleased about this but then commented rather wistfully, 'You know, though, I was much more interested in mathematics and electronics than I was in psychology. Even though I was good at maths, my school told me when I was in Standard 7 that maths was not for blind people, and I was forced to give it up. That's why I'm a psychologist and not a scientist.'

3

Nothing About Them

A few years ago, I attended a meeting at which disability researchers and activists were working to establish some disability research in southern Africa. The meeting was held in a hotel in Gaborone, Botswana, during midsummer. The hotel had double-booked, so our meeting was relegated to a large tent in the garden of the hotel. There were feeble attempts to keep us cool – large noisy fans, and some water sprays – but we were condemned to the heat. Many of the African delegates wore jackets and ties, as is customary, and though they sweated and sweated, the jackets and ties stayed put. The delegates represented disabled people's organisations, and had a wide range of activist experience. Some delegates had completed school and had tertiary education, but some had not.

Every day we were given the typical lunch one has at such meetings: lots of meat, vegetables, watery salad, rice and sadza, or mielie-meal porridge, one of my favourite foods, which I'd learnt to enjoy as a child when our servants in what was then Rhodesia had shared their food with us. I was helping one of the delegates, a wheelchair user sweating in his black suit, to get his lunch, and we were chatting about this and that. A major topic in the news at the time was the ascendance of creationism and the concept of 'intelligent design' in the USA, a product of right-wing religious ideology which gained support during the George W. Bush presidency. As a researcher (and I was attending this meeting as a researcher), I was appalled by what was happening in the USA around the teaching of 'intelligent design' in school classrooms, including visits to museums with fake exhibits to rival scientifically based museums of natural history. Before I could comment, though, my colleague looked up at me from his wheelchair and said, 'I don't like this evolution stuff. It says I come from monkeys and baboons. I am not a baboon!' Eager to make a good impression on the gathering and to be accepted as a researcher among a group of disabled people, I did not argue; I took the cowardly way out and changed the subject. But I got to thinking about the delegate's remarks and their meaning in a context very different from my own world of academia, and from the world of George Bush and his right-wing cronies.

When I was growing up in Rhodesia (we left shortly after Ian Smith's Unilateral Declaration of Independence from Britain in 1965), it was not uncommon for white Rhodesians to call black people 'apes' or 'baboons'. This practice was not confined to Rhodesia. A joke doing the rounds when South African prime minister B.J. Vorster met Zambian president Kenneth Kaunda in 1976 went as follows:

B.J. Vorster, the Queen of England and Kenneth Kaunda were all at a high-level meeting. When the Queen got up to speak, the band played 'God Save the Queen'. Then it was Vorster's turn to speak, and the band played 'Die Stem van Suid-Afrika' [the then South African national anthem]. At last it was Kaunda's turn to speak. The band played 'Bobbejaan Klim die Berg'.

'Bobbejaan Klim die Berg' ('Baboon climbs the mountain') is a traditional Afrikaans song about a baboon who bothers the (Afrikaner) farmers.

The mistaken implication of evolutionary theory that we are all related to, or descended from, baboons has a different meaning in the context of a history of racism where black people are viewed as baboons. In the history of medicine and psychiatry, a crude abuse of evolutionary theory can be seen in many forms. For example, for a long time psychiatrists believed that there was no depression in Africa or among 'primitive' people, because these people lacked the insight to feel depressed: they were happy-go-lucky savages living in the present, unlike more complex and civilised humans. All credible scientific work on this subject has found this assertion, which was once the dominant view, to be false.[1] Similarly, few people have not seen so-called Darwinist drawings of heads where African people are labelled as a transition in evolutionary terms between apes and humans; such drawings have been unfairly used by creationists to attack all aspects of Darwinism. For an African to want to dissociate himself from any theory which implies that he (and all of us) may be related to baboons is understandable.

But this delegate was not just a black African man. He was also a disabled African man – a wheelchair user. Disabled people have been viewed as not really human, but as animals, or even as 'vegetables', a term sometimes used to talk about people with intellectual disability in particular. This 'vegetable' label is used to great comic effect by a downloadable radio show on 'Ouch!', the BBC's disability website. One of the popular programmes on the show is called 'Vegetable, Vegetable or Vegetable', in which listeners can phone in and presenters have to guess the person's impairment. But does this rather wonderful spoof on the game 'Animal, Vegetable or Mineral' have a different meaning in Britain than in some parts of Africa? Could it be that anxiety about being called a 'baboon' may be based in a reality in which such name-calling is not as remote as in Britain, where people have learnt to be more careful about what they say (even if they think no differently)? I think this is so. There's also another layer to this, a layer which was brought home to me at the same meeting.

Some of the dynamics of the meeting were very familiar to people involved in development work in Africa. On the one hand were our European funders (all of them white), with their laptops and their earnest attempts to be culturally and politically sensitive. On the other were the African delegates (most, but not all, of them black), with their vast experience of development work and activism on the continent; they were extremely articulate on issues of activism, but much less versed in the now international language of logframe analysis, project management and research methodologies. At this meeting, however, and at some other disability meetings like it, there is the other cross-cutting dimension of disability. At such meetings, a European with an impairment that is the same as that of an African delegate may be seen, social model or no social model, context or no context, to be understanding something about the experience of that African delegate. Is there a kind of insider knowledge which all people who have impairments share, which the rest of us don't have access to?

I don't have much problem answering 'yes' to this question, because of my own experience. When I think about and try to understand my father's life, for example, I know that though I lived with him and loved him for many years, there are things I couldn't know about living with his strange body. I saw him in pain, but I never felt that pain; I saw his absolute determination and judged it from my perspective, but I would never know what it was like to have that determination in the face of a body which in important ways had let him and let his family down. From a very young age, I noticed the flicker of confusion, of pity and at times of revulsion on the faces of people who met my father for the first time and saw his awkward limp, or his bare feet with twisted toes when he was on the beach. I also saw the quiet, well-mannered (and socially completely appropriate) second of effort in the faces of those who were surprised: 'I'm not going to mention this,' their faces would say. 'I'm going to look at the person beyond this.' I noticed all this out of care for my father and concern for myself as his child, but I have no idea what it must feel like, day in and day out, to have a body that others read and react to as different. I don't know what it's like to have a body other people have to decide to look beyond. And this separates me from people with physical impairments and from my own father. As I write this, I hear in my head voices of family members saying, 'But you're making too much of this – it really didn't matter, and certainly not to your dad.' I feel bad, guilty myself, for saying that it did matter – this feels in some way like a betrayal of my father and of his strength. But pretending, along with so many other people, that

43

it's possible 'not to notice' and not to react to an impairment feels to me to be much worse – like a kind of conspiracy against a reality that disabled people must live with. I know I react to impairment – I notice it. And I don't want to align myself with the kind of denial of the lived experience of disability that to me is very similar to a denial implicit in comments of well-meaning white people who say of their interactions with black people, 'I don't see colour.' Are you blind, I want to say, and even if you were blind, you'd probably read many colour cues in a host of other ways, through accents and ways of talking and so on. And what if my dad said what I'm talking about doesn't exist? That I imagined people looked at him differently because of his impairments? Well, sorry, Dad, I still think I'm right (as I always did in my fights with him to be and become my own man), but let's put this argument on hold for a bit while I go back to telling another story from that same meeting in the very hot tent that very hot summer.

One of the more powerful delegates at the meeting was a well-known European disability studies activist and researcher. I'd been warned independently by a number of people, both disabled and able-bodied, that this man was good at what he did, but he could be rude, especially to able-bodied people like me. When I saw what appeared to me to be his very mild impairment and a limp far less pronounced than my father's, I am ashamed to say that part of me thought, unforgivably, 'Well, you aren't really very disabled at all, are you? What right do you have to claim to be disabled?' It is interesting, though embarrassing, that in order to defuse a potential threat from a stern disability activist, in my mind I was using exactly the same kind of crude distinctions between the disabled and the non-disabled that I myself was so critical of! Perhaps because I caught myself at this and was a bit ashamed of myself, I was on the lookout for something more acceptable to criticise him about. And I got what I was looking for.

I have a colleague and friend, a white South African woman, who has no visible disability, and who is very well liked in disability circles in South Africa and a number of low-income countries. She gave a talk at the meeting in which she discussed the need for improved services for disabled people in southern Africa. As soon as she had finished her talk, the European disability activist, whom I'll call Tomas, said, 'As disabled people, we want rights; we want equality. We don't want your services. Stop talking about services.' His tone was aggressive, and it was as though my colleague had committed an act of great violence against disabled people through her saying that services were needed. In effect he was commanding this able-bodied researcher to shut up, not to talk about what she knew.

There are many ways of thinking about this interaction. First off, let's get out of the way that there are rude people in the world, some able-bodied and some disabled. And Tomas is rude. His reputation precedes him. This has nothing necessarily to do with disability issues. But despite the fact that many disabled African people commonly speak loudly and assertively about what they believe to be right, nobody questioned Tomas at the meeting, or tried to mediate or soften his words. We must allow for the possibility that people who knew Tomas had learnt that there was simply no point in contradicting him – that you would get nowhere questioning this self-appointed expert. But I, at least, should have said something (I am often known for my big mouth), yet I said nothing either. Why? In part, I was simply relieved that my colleague was the one getting flak and that it was not me (and the gender dimensions of her being attacked, as opposed to me, who knows much less than she does about the field, were not lost on me). I was also afraid, scared to say anything that could be heard as criticism, not of Tomas himself, but of disabled people in general. I was afraid to be seen as disablist, in the same way that as a white South African man I don't want to be seen as racist or sexist. But Tomas was talking what to me, if not to him, seemed to be utter nonsense, and I left what he said unchallenged. This was, I admit, not very brave of me.

I knew then and I know now that what he was saying was either wilfully or mistakenly ignorant, and I am not sure which is worse. In that hot tent were people who have been excluded from education, from health care, from getting appropriate assistive devices – we did not even have to look further than that very group of disabled people, a group which by virtue of being there was more privileged than most disabled people in Africa, to know that access to services is a major concern for disabled people. Writing in a book which I helped co-edit some years ago, Nokwanele Mgwili spoke movingly about her difficulties as a wheelchair user in accessing adequate reproductive health services.[2] Not for a moment do I think that she was making this up, nor do I think that her experience was at all unusual. Parents struggle, too, to get education for their disabled children, and adult education is also difficult for disabled people to access.[3] In Europe and North America, where, despite continuing difficulties, many of the wars about services have been won, it is easy to reject service provision as an old 'medical model' way of confusing disability rights with a kind of patronising welfarism, in which disabled people are seen to be vulnerable and in need of care from able-bodied professionals. There's much to recommend this view, a view which has gained credibility in part because of the success of generations of struggle by disabled people. But in Africa, things are different.

So there we all sat, cowardly to the very last one of us, allowing my colleague (who, luckily, is very resilient) to be railed at unfairly by Tomas, who was giving his own views but not, as far as I could work out, the views of anyone else at the meeting. As I sat there I was reminded of the early days of the progressive health movement in South Africa in the 1980s. These were exciting days, in which we were overturning what we had known about professionalism and health care in South Africa. We were interested in access to health care for all South Africans, and we were training community members to do things that many had thought they could not do: to provide a range of cheap and effective health promotion, prevention and curative services. We were critical of our own privilege and of our assumption that only professionals could do community work. At one of our national meetings, we were addressed by a well-known trade unionist. His speech was a tirade against us as whites (most of us at the meeting, though not all of us, were white) and as professionals: 'You bloody professionals,' he said. 'You whiteys, you know nothing – nothing at all – about what the people need! You don't care. You are all so privileged, and all you care about are your fancy houses and your swimming pools and your BMWs!' And so on and so on. Now we were the very professionals who were trying to do something different with our work, who were spending hours and hours doing unpaid community work, so the unionist was not altogether accurate. But what did we do in response to his tirade? We clapped, we whistled, we cheered. There was something about his insults that made us feel that at last we were in the real world, face to face with real black anger, not protected by our racial and professional privilege. This was the real thing, the coalface of struggle, just where we needed to be!

It's easy with the benefit of over twenty years' hindsight to question our enthusiasm for being abused as progressive health-care workers at that time. We now know how in many ways professional health-care organisations have retreated to important degrees from cutting-edge community work, and that the quest for the BMW and ostentatious displays of wealth has become a feature of the emergent (mainly black) professional and middle class in South Africa. But there was something exhilarating then about being shouted at by a real live trade unionist, when many of us had never seen a trade unionist before. We learnt something about politics and about the power of political positioning – not an altogether bad lesson, and one which perhaps justifies our rather silly acceptance of, or our revelling in, the unfair abuse we were taking.

Is there a link between this story of the trade unionist abusing progressive health workers in the South Africa of the 1980s and the way in which we Africans allowed Tomas, the European disability activist, what was apparently yet another moment of imposing his will on an African meeting? I think there is a link. In both scenarios we have a political movement (whether of mainly white health professionals in 1980s South Africa or of disability activists in southern Africa in the 2000s), a movement which needs credibility and cohesion. In the 1980s we progressive health workers needed a sense of an organic link to the 'real life' of the majority working class in South Africa, and an obnoxious trade unionist fitted the bill much more snugly than a polite person would have done, a person who could so easily have been labelled a 'sell-out', toadying up to the professionals. And what did we have in Tomas in the disability meeting? We had, in a nutshell, the good old social model, and the powerful politics of disability identity.

The authority Tomas used to make his statements about what disabled people need in southern Africa, and his use of the pronoun 'we', implied that he was part of a group on whose behalf he had a right to speak. Before we go any further, let's imagine Tomas was an able-bodied white European man speaking at a meeting of mainly black African people. If at a meeting like that he had referred to 'we' and 'what we want', he would have been in trouble – people would have accused him of being patronising, of colonialist arrogance, for assuming he could speak for Africans. I've seen this kind of criticism of well-meaning (and sometimes bemused) Europeans many times. So how did Tomas get away with what he did? I think his authority came directly from his having a body with an impairment. He would probably dispute this claim; he would say that as a disabled person (disabled, in the social-model sense, by society) he understands from the inside what disablist oppression is – that there must be links between what he has gone through and what African disabled people go through. So far so good; I think he's probably right. But how far do the similarities go? Life in Europe is for the most part very different from life in Africa. All sorts of assumptions are made,

I think, that the body of this disabled person, the impairment, confers an authority, a special insider knowledge, on all disabled people. To my mind, these assumptions are actually in violation of the social model, which says that impairment is in fact less important than are social barriers and the experience of oppression – all of which are very much dependent on context. But the authority of the bodily impairment remains, social model or no social model.

One of the central slogans of the international disability movement is 'Nothing about us without us', and what a great slogan it is. It captures in a few words the rights of disabled people to speak for themselves, not to be spoken about by patronising professionals or by people who think they know better than disabled people about what is good for disabled people. Self-representation is at the heart of any credible liberation movement, as feminists and black consciousness activists have well understood. But in the 'Nothing about us without us' statement, the idea of 'us' is not simple. I don't think that having an impairment is enough to allow anyone to speak for other people in very different circumstances and contexts. The maturing international feminist movement has been very good at showing us how important it is to pay attention to differences in people's context and life circumstances. Though all women may share some experiences, no European feminist today would get away with claiming to speak on behalf of a group of African women unless she had negotiated this very, very carefully. In a similar way, I don't think Tomas had an unproblematic right to speak on behalf of disabled people in Africa. I might not have even thought this through, though, had I agreed with Tomas and found him personable and pleasant. But this is my own failing:

I too sometimes attribute far too much to the impairment itself, automatically allowing authority to anybody with an impairment.

But what about me in all this? What rights do I have to speak? I suppose if I am quite honest I am claiming some knowledge about disabled people and their needs in my context which I don't think Tomas shares. I wouldn't try to speak on behalf of disabled people in South Africa or anywhere else. Or would I? Aren't I trying to do just that? Well, in some senses, you've got me – I do want to say things, things that other people (including disabled people) aren't saying. More important in some ways, though, is that this book feels very personal – it feels like a story about my heart, my blood, my being. But in planning to do it, and through the utter joy and relief in writing it, I have in my head all sorts of voices and faces of people saying, 'You are not allowed to do this.' As I said in the first chapter, some of these voices are those of my family or of people who care for my family – in writing about them, about my father in particular, with love, I also do violence. But there's another layer to this. In writing in what I hope is a respectful way about disability politics, writing with what I hope is respect and, yes, one could even say a kind of love, similar to the love I feel for my family, am I doing something terrible at the same time? I know there are some people who won't be happy with this book, and for some of them it will not be the content of the book that is the problem. It is the fact of my choosing as an able-bodied person to write my own book about disabled people from my own perspective. To these critics, the very fact of my writing this book violates the 'Nothing about us ...' principle. I may protest, defensively, that I've done a lot and continue to do a lot of work together with disabled people, and this book is a special book for me. But I don't think that would wash with everyone. I have to live with the contradictions between my wanting to do something which is mine, something which is helpful in terms of disability, and the reality that I claim – because of all my privileges – an authority and a right to do this. And I do claim it.

One of the most hurtful things a student ever said about my teaching was communicated to me very recently. I had taught a course which was not about disability, but because I feel so strongly about disability issues I dragged disability into this course, kicking and screaming (as I do with most of my courses). We have a nice word for this – we call it 'mainstreaming' disability issues – but 'dragging in' may be a bit more accurate! In this course I showed my students (none of whom had a visible impairment) a set of slides I've collected on how disabled people are, or are not, represented in the media. I think most of the students enjoyed the presentation, but one of my students wrote the following as part of the anonymous written feedback process: 'The worst session on the course was the one on disability – whatever any-one tries to do is wrong. I am tired of political correctness.' I felt hurt by the comment because it told me that in the case of this student at least I had failed to communicate anything of use. I was trying to give a complex argument, one based on experience, and to help students to think more, and more deeply, about disability. But to this student I was trying to do the opposite of helping people to think – I was trying to straitjacket thinking in a 'politically correct' framework. And there is a huge danger that real concerns about participation, about people speaking for themselves, about long and difficult struggles for autonomy, can be reduced to a trivial policing of what we are allowed to say without getting into trouble. Am I guilty of this? I hope not, but I have to accept that my student feels otherwise.

These things are just so difficult. On the one hand, how we use words is truly important. It matters that people have understood that in the language we use we show, often unintentionally, whom we are including as important and excluding as irrelevant. I am old enough to remember the early feminist struggles for non-sexist language in the 1960s and 1970s, and I do think it makes a difference whether we say 'All men are created equal' or 'All people are created equal'. At the same time, I remember the insightful discussion by my friend Valerie Sinason[4] of how, because of our anxiety and worry about intellectual disability, we keep changing the name for it in a kind of hope that magically the new words will change the ongoing reality. And I baulk at what I see as silly attempts to control the way we talk about things without thinking about the bigger context. I got an email recently from a student at a South African university (not my own) who is in the early stages of establishing a disabled students' society. This student, who is herself disabled, mentioned to me that even the name of the society she is hoping to get going is being hotly disputed. One staff member, for example, told the student that she should use the word 'impairment' rather than 'disability' in the name of the society. My heart sank at this simple-mindedness, which I guessed probably came from a very earnest social-model adherent. I could hear in my head all the reasons why the staff member had made this suggestion, but who of the general university population (including most disabled students) will know about or care about all the arguments about the difference between 'disability' and 'impairment'? And if

we are wanting to do activism around disability issues, it must surely be important to use language people will recognise even if the
language may not be perfect (and language, sad to say, never is).

The student starting the society commented very thoughtfully
in a follow-up email: 'I must be honest – the issue of naming gives
me a headache. I really feel that in so many cases the disabled aren't
given the opportunity to choose and that often the harsh reality
of an individual's situation is swept under the carpet by a name
that makes everyone feel more comfortable.' What an irony that
the issue of naming and how we talk about disability has become,
for this student anyway, a new way of controlling what can and
can't be said – 'the disabled aren't given the opportunity to choose,'
as she says. And she makes a further important point: disability
activism, like all activism, should be about making us uncomfortable, confronting us with questions, forcing us to think, making
us face difficult issues. But in her experience there is something
going on in all this so-called activism which has become a kind
of hiding away of things, of sweeping things under the carpet, of
making us comfortable. I think this student has a point in what
she says. All political movements, when they become the new
orthodoxies, can become comfortable havens of in-group mutual
support, where others are excluded and difficult things ignored.
This is not unique to disability. But I want to take up this student's challenge. And (in a self-serving way, I know) I want to say
that this book is partly an attempt to think aloud about the new
orthodoxies in the disability studies world and to take them on.
The fact that I am writing the book at all is already a challenge
to think more and differently about things than an easy (and false)
radicalism can allow.

4

Growing Up Painfully

I am the youngest of a large brood of cousins on my mother's side. To some extent this large number of cousins makes up for the lack of cousins on my father's side. For quite a few of my teenage years, I was friendly with my eldest cousin. Dinky is about eighteen years older than me (the same gap as between my mother and her eldest sister, Auntie Tilly). Dinky had married very young, and her eldest son, David, is about a year younger than me. Dinky was (and is) dazzling, intelligent and outspoken, and the only person I remember standing up squarely to the Buchenwald Chicken, an event that stands out in my memory.

In South Africa's pre-television days, it was a treat for us to be invited to Dinky's house to watch a movie on a loud and cumbersome 18-mm projector. The movie we watched on that memorable night was *Planet of the Apes* – the original 1968 version starring Charlton Heston. I found the film enthralling, but Auntie Leah did not like it at all, and she began to complain loudly about the film and its poor quality. Such was her power that others of us might have let her continue in this vein, but Dinky was having none of it. She stopped the film and said, 'Leah [it's significant that

Dinky said 'Leah' and not 'Lea'], we are enjoying the film and you are not. You are rude to spoil everyone else's fun. Either stay here and be quiet, or go and make yourself a cup of tea in the kitchen.' Auntie Leah shut up immediately, and I remember this being the first time in my life that I had consciously thought of an adult as being rude.

Dinky was known in the family for her forthrightness and her ability to upset people at times, and on this night all of us except Auntie Leah benefited from this. But Dinky was also under much strain. Her daughter, Ruth, was lying in bed in traction and was in a lot of pain with the weights hanging down at the end of the bed. I don't remember how Ruth's joint problems started, but we now know that Ruth suffers from Gaucher's disease (as does her brother David, though he experienced much later onset). Gaucher's is an inherited metabolic disorder which is rare but more common in Jews of Ashkenazi (Eastern European) origin. There are many signs and symptoms, but among the earliest symptoms one can get is severe bone pain, which Ruth had. At that time, Ruth's diagnosis of Gaucher's had not been made, but for years she lived with a great deal of pain and anguish. When we think about disability and illness, we often think of these as the only, or the defining, features of people's lives; yet this is never true, just as it was not the case in Ruth's life. Dinky had married young and her marriage was not a happy one. Her divorce, after three children, was protracted and unpleasant. Part of why it was so difficult for both Dinky and her ex-husband was that divorce, in our extended family at any rate, was rare and considered scandalous, and they stayed together probably much longer than they should have, much to their own unhappiness and that of their children. (By the time of my own divorce many years later, at least one child of every one of my mother's siblings who had children had either been divorced or had gone through very public marital difficulties, so things were a lot easier for me.) I never felt I got to know Ruth well, but she seemed to me at that time to be unhappy quite apart from her joint problems. She was very beautiful in an ethereal, Pre-Raphaelite sort of way, and bookish and clever, but she had a lot to deal with as a child. Her illness and her physical pain formed only part of the story, but how could it not be that her experience of these was impacted by all the other concerns (and joys) of her young life? Conversely, her physical pain affected the rest of her life. It was the heyday of very psychologised views about pain and suffering, and it took many years for Ruth to be diagnosed with Gaucher's. So for that time she also had to bear the silent but powerful views of many that all of this pain was somehow made up, that she was 'looking for attention', that all this was 'really' about her parents' failures and their divorce. Ruth was somehow to blame and so was her mother.

I never once saw Dinky disavow what was going on with Ruth, much to Dinky's credit. Nor did I hear people blaming Dinky or Ruth in their presence or behind their backs. But this was the message. Nasty things happen around illness and pain. First, people can see them as just deserts for bad actions ('look what Ruth's going through because of Dinky's messy divorce'). Second, people are judged for having pain, and especially pain that won't go away when the doctors try to put it right. What we too often fail to see, even when people may in part be 'looking for attention', is that if a child like Ruth would go to such lengths to 'look for attention', she must be very desperate. We don't want people to be ill and not get well – it frightens us, reminds us of our own vulnerabilities. If we can find a way to blame sick people for their illness, then we get magically protected. This is so not just for illness and disability, but for all difficult and tragic things. We also need coherent stories, small morality tales, to make us feel better. A few years ago, when two young men in Cape Town were hijacked in their car and brutally murdered by gangsters, two competing stories immediately began to circulate. One was that the young men were killed because they were Jewish; the other was that they were killed because they were gay. In the trial that followed it was clearly shown that these young men were simply and tragically in the wrong place at the wrong time, but that is in some ways a much more scary thought than 'they were killed because …'

Dinky adored my father, and I think it's fair to say that was partly because he did not judge her as others did, but also because in his own irascible way he paid her the compliment of always being honest with her. He was critical of a lot of what she did and he made this clear. He told her what he thought. The only thing I don't remember his telling her about was his critical attitude towards her children and their attitudes towards health and illness. When Dinky was still married and we were living in Rhodesia, we went to see the family at Salisbury airport. They were on their way to Britain where Syd, Dinky's husband, was to specialise as a pathologist, and Salisbury airport was a stop on the way. At the time David and Ruth were both young children, and their little brother Jonty was an adorable toddler. Understandably, David was tired and grumpy from travelling and he had a headache. He asked his mother for some Panado for his headache. My father said nothing at the time but he was appalled. On the way home he angrily blurted out, 'Did you hear how those children know the names of pills and medicines? It's disgusting.' This was to be an ongoing theme in my father's relationship with Dinky and her children. He believed that children should not know too much about illness and drugs, because this knowledge encouraged them to manufacture illnesses, to complain about their bodies, and to become weak and difficult. As the years went by, especially after we moved to Johannesburg and saw them more often, my father's displeasure grew and grew. Ruth had become seriously ill and could recite a range of drugs, and David and Jonty also knew about medication.

One day when Ruth was in traction and in a lot of pain, my father went into her room. She was inconsolable and, after a few minutes, my father said gruffly, 'Well, I had much worse traction than this – much heavier weights and for much longer.' This was probably true – my father had been through the mill as far as pain and painful treatments were concerned – but how was it that this kind man, who was loved by many and who cared a lot for vulnerable people, could be so short with someone in pain? His implication to Ruth was that her distress and her discomfort were not legitimate, that she had no right to be behaving this way. I saw a sad young girl in agony and afraid; my father saw some-body who was spoilt and making too much of her difficulties. There was something quite complicated going on here, I think, because the gruffness and refusal to acknowledge how difficult Ruth was finding things was also a way of trying to make it better: if my dad could just convince Ruth that what was happening was not serious, or was something that could be survived, perhaps she would feel better. There was another level to this too. My father's pain and physical difficulties had never been his own; they were never allowed to be. Any pain he might have had was translated immediately into an added burden for his poor mother. In his life, especially growing up, any weakness he felt, any pain, any need for help and care, quickly became a way in which his mother could show him how hard her life was, what a burden he was, how much she had gone through. Was he trying, perhaps, to help Ruth be less of a burden, to be less vulnerable to being made to pay tenfold for the misery she was causing her own mother? I think so. So in the gruffness and harshness there was a kind of gift, but one which I did not get at the time and I don't think Ruth did either.

I wonder also about my father's strong feelings about the way in which Ruth and her siblings talked about their medicines. I'm not saying he did not have a point with his worry about their being too indulged and medicated – there are enough books around these days that talk about these kinds of problems in generations of middle-class children. But could there have been something else in his irritability with these children and their medication, and with Ruth in her pain? Whatever Dinky's faults might have been, and whatever mistakes she might have made in bringing up her children (and we all make lots of mistakes), one thing Dinky was able to do was to listen attentively when her children were in distress, to discuss their aches and pains with them, and to give them some sense that there were things out there that might help them with their pain. My grandmother could do none of this. All my father's ailments and his physical difficulties were weapons she turned back on him ('I walked the floor with you!' – the pain of her endless nights spent trying to soothe her broken child). I myself was well acquainted with Granny as an operator. 'Don't break your granny's heart' was the refrain for anything she didn't want me to do. Anything she didn't like would break her and kill her, and anyway she had such a short time left on this earth ('I'll be pushing up daisies!') that it would be cruel to do anything to disturb her. In the event, I did do many things that could be classified as Capable of Breaking Granny's Heart, as did my father, and she survived them all, even outliving my father by many years. But the story, and the demand, were always there.

When I think about my father and Ruth, then, I wonder whether there was a part of him that envied her, not for many things, and certainly not for her chronic condition and her on-going pain, but for the fact that her illness was not thrown back at her as a reprimand, as a burden to her mother. He had been forced to go subterranean with so many parts of his life, including his pain, partly because that's what men of his generation had to do, but partly to stop his mother from getting in there and turning what he was going through into a high drama of her own, stealing his pain and his right to feelings. It must have been unbearable to see Ruth being cared for as she was cared for, so he reprimanded her, told her that things were not so bad. This came about not because he didn't care, but possibly because he cared too much.

And, of course, my father had an authority that none of the rest of us had. Our family, as it happens, is littered with hip problems: Auntie Tilly and her rolling gait; Auntie Ada (Dinky's mother and Ruth's grandmother) and her three – count 'em, three – hip replacements (she was really unlucky and one replacement was for a broken femur); and even Dinky hurt her hip in an accident. But my father had had traction and had been a very sickly baby. So when he asserted what was wrong or not wrong with Ruth, he had a unique, insider authority. He did not have to claim this authority for himself; it was assumed by all and just given to him. Years later, when thinking about the 'Nothing about us without us' slogan of the disability movement, I remembered my father's insider authority and recognised it, but I also wondered about the complexity of it all.

In the previous chapter I discussed some of the challenges associated with the idea of the 'us' of the disability movement, and we've seen how the use of 'us' can massage away, or hide, important differences and conflicts among disabled people. But there's an added problem. Just like everyone else, every disabled person (including people who become disabled later in life) grows up in his or her own particular way, with his or her own particular family drama. And these experiences colour the lives of all of us, disability or no disability. Like my father, we may then want to police the behaviour and feelings of others in accordance with our own expectations and experience. I'm making this sound much too sinister, and it isn't. When we meet people who we think are like us (or are different from us), we make assumptions about them, about their experiences, about the similarities and differences between us. When we share a political identity (such as oppressed or disabled), we may have quite a lot invested in our stories converging, in our having essentially the same stories to tell. So far, so good. But when we overlook that this kind of process is happening, when we don't think about it, we may soon develop a way of dealing with others we see as similar to ourselves which enforces certain ways of being and disallows others. My father had trouble allowing Ruth to be weak; others may have trouble with disabled people not feeling oppressed, or not feeling let down by able-bodied people. And there can even be rules about how people must experience their impairments and deal with them, as I learnt from Brian Watermeyer.

As I've discussed in Chapter 2, Brian has a progressive and deteriorating visual impairment. He grew up sighted and is slowly losing his vision. Legally he is blind, but he can see enough to get around most of the time without the use of a cane or a guide dog, or any of the trappings that we associate with blind people. He also has all the non-verbal ways of interacting that we associate with sighted people: he looks at you when you talk and participates in the subtle rules of gaze which we recognise only when they are broken, as they sometimes are by people who have grown up blind and have not learnt this complex visual dance. Some people who have no visual impairment do not believe that Brian has any visual problems at all – they suspect he must be 'making it up' – or they forget about the visual impairment, as he does not 'look blind' in any way. Surely, the implicit story goes, if he were 'really' blind, he'd have all the trappings of blindness? But, interestingly enough, it's not only able-bodied people who treat him in this way. Some people with visual impairments similar to his own berate him for not using a cane or a guide dog, and argue that he is 'in denial' about his impairment. The 'in denial' allegation is always a trump card – I have no doubt that it is possible for people to be 'in denial', but I also know that once you accuse someone of being in denial, there's not much they can do about it, as you are claiming access to what's really going on with them when they don't have this access. (Freud's got a lot to answer for!) And even if Brian is indeed 'in denial', it surely can't be by chance that what people who make this claim about him want most is for him to be just like them. If he toed the line in terms of disability identity and behaviour, they probably wouldn't be saying he's in denial at all (though he could be, about a whole host of things, as we all are!).

So, 'Nothing about us ...' isn't just about solidarity in any simple sense; it's also about who we want other people to be so that we can have our own identity confirmed. But things can get even more complicated when it comes to the politics of self-representation under conditions of oppression. We all have parts of ourselves which cause us difficulties, which we'd rather be rid of. This is part of being human. It is often the case that we put these parts of ourselves into others so we do not have to deal with them as part of us. Tom Shakespeare has accurately shown how disabled people can come to serve as what he calls 'dustbins for disavowal' for the parts of able-bodied people that we don't want to deal with.[1] Instead of accepting and dealing with the fact that we all have parts of ourselves that feel weak or ugly or badly put together, we can see these characteristics as being unique to disabled people. If 'they' are the weak ones, the ugly ones, the malformed ones, we don't have to deal with our own weakness, ugliness, malformation. Disabled people have to fight these processes every day, just as in different ways black people ('they are all smelly, lazy, stupid') and women ('they are all weak, hysterical, devious') have had to do the same. It is essential that disabled people keep pointing out the pernicious folly of these attributions. Paradoxically, though, one of the effects that fighting these stereotypes may have is that disabled people may want to police themselves and other disabled people into not being what others think they are. I believe that all of us, including all disabled people, have parts of ourselves that we believe to be weak, ugly, malformed, hysterical, devious, smelly, lazy or stupid, to name just a few. But when these are the names we are called (or silently whispered), these are the names we fight against and may want others like us to fight against. My father grew up being told in no uncertain terms that he was a worry and a burden, and he spent the rest of his life trying to prove in various ways that he wasn't. Part of what he couldn't bear about Ruth was that whatever else she was going through, she seemed to have little trouble being a worry and a burden to her mother: she was not 'brave'; she found no need to hide her pain. In similar ways, disabled people may be pulled into policing the behaviour of other disabled people because this is what is seen as necessary in order to fight a bigger oppression – the oppression of being, as a group, 'dustbins' of the type Tom Shakespeare describes.

There are positive consequences, then, to sticking together for solidarity, but there are costs. I was recently one of a group of South African Jews who sent a letter to the *South African Jewish Report* criticising the ferocity of Israel's attacks on Gaza in early 2009. There was a flurry of correspondence condemning this letter, all from Jews who supported Israel's actions. In these letters, we were condemned as 'ignorant' and 'apologetic', and as 'so-called Jews'. One letter writer said ominously, 'We do not need any Jewish "quislings" in our midst.' Flattered in a perverse way though I am to be called a traitor, what I think is going on here is relevant to thinking about disability identity. I don't want to get into any arguments here about who's right and who's wrong about Israel and Gaza, or about whether my and my co-signatories' views were correctly understood. The important point is that when a group feels under enormous pressure and threat, as the letter writers to the *South African Jewish Report* do, and understandably so, there is a tendency to see all difference and debate within the group as insanity, suicide or treachery, to use some very strong terms. The price of solidarity may be that of conformity. In some respects this is not a problem in a movement which people join solely on the basis of common beliefs, but it becomes much more problematic when the movement is organised around a given identity – like a Jewish identity in my case, or a disabled identity. The policing may then become not just a policing on the basis of beliefs, but a policing of who you are.

I was reminded about this issue of identity politics when I started working with a very prominent disability activist some years ago. This person has done a huge amount of good for the disability movement and continues to do so. But his relationship to other disabled people cannot be described as uncomplicated. We first met when I was planning to do some research in collaboration with the disability movement. I struggled for months to get hold of the people from the movement I wanted to consult about the work and was about to give up the project altogether when I got a phone call from this man, who did not pause to ask me what I had done to contact the movement but instead told me in very clear terms that what I had been doing was 'very wrong' – that I had not been trying to consult with the movement and this would not do. When I described to him the work we were planning, including a long period of consultation workshops, he said, 'But why are you bothering to have these workshops – you have spoken to me!' It was true that he had been delegated authority by the disability movement, but in his mind he was completely identified with it – to speak to him alone was to speak to the movement. It's easy to dismiss this as arrogance, but I don't think it is that. When people are accustomed to speaking on behalf of others, and to sharing their group identity, they make the same mistake we all make – asking the one black person in the room, for example, to give 'the black perspective'. When I came to Stellenbosch University there were very few Jews around (there still are), and suddenly I became the representative and spokes-person for all things Jewish. I was even asked by a colleague on one occasion, 'Do you have *braaivleis* in your Jewish culture?' – a question at once endearing in its openness and revealing of the split world within which even white South Africans live. My disabled colleague, time and again, had been 'the disabled rep' on hundreds of committees, and the effects were beginning to tell.

Interestingly, as we worked together my disabled colleague revealed more of these identity issues. He took it upon himself to 'explain' disabled people to me and my able-bodied colleagues, sometimes in terms that were less than flattering. He would say, for example, 'Don't expect disabled people to organise themselves very well – they just can't do it,' or 'Don't give them too many choices – just be firm with them.' Could there be something here similar to what I saw in my father about wanting to seem different from a complaining weakling, a caricature of disability? I think so, but I also think the easy authority of being part of the bigger disability movement allowed this kind of talk. If I as an able-bodied person were to say these sorts of things about disabled people, I'd be in big trouble – and some of the big trouble would come from this activist himself! There's a funny kind of paradox here, but an important one. On the one hand, a disabled activist in an able-bodied world has to stand for and on behalf of all other disabled people: 'Nothing about us without us'. But in having to play this role, a disabled person in an able-bodied world also has to be different from the people he or she is representing – there is a need here to act as a kind of broker or interpreter, to claim the authority not just as a disabled person but also as a person who knows about disabled people.

But being an interpreter or a culture broker is not an easy thing. When I was working in a large psychiatric hospital, where nurses often took the role of interpreters for Xhosa-speaking patients, I learnt something about these complexities.[2] On the surface, the role of an interpreter in health care is quite simple. The interpreter must translate what the patient says so the doctor can understand, and must also translate what the doctor says so the patient can understand. But there are also all sorts of less obvious messages about what interpreters must do. For example, they must 'stand for' or represent people to the health system. I saw nurses cringe when asked to interpret for rude and angry patients, feeling embarrassed at what they would have to translate, not just because the patients were rude and angry, but because, especially in apartheid South Africa, the nurses were seen as black people 'just like the patients'. I understand some Xhosa and I could see that nurses often did not interpret accurately what patients were saying, especially when patients were very rude or swore. They often made things sound better – made the patients seem more polite and less 'crazy'. Sometimes, though, they would do the opposite; they would say things like, 'He is a very low-class type of person, not a good sort, not respectable.' By saying this, nurses would be making it clear that they were not the sort of person the patient was, the sort of person who could create a bad impression in the minds of white doctors.

My colleague and friend Hester van der Walt also has a nursing background, and in a chapter in a book I co-edited she tells a similar story.[3] In her own work as a community nurse in working-class areas of South Africa, she found it relatively easy to empathise with the difficulties experienced by poor black South Africans. When dealing with poor white South Africans (Hester is a white South African herself), she often found herself being judgemental and angry with her clients, blaming them for their poverty and their health difficulties. She wanted to distance herself from these people, and to get away from being what she called 'too close for comfort'. At first she did not think too much about this, but when she was working as a researcher in the tuberculosis field she started to see similar things with nurses in the TB-control programme. She saw coloured nurses being harsh to coloured patients they saw as coming from their own communities, but being understanding to patients who were white or black African and seen as different from themselves. And this happened with nurses from other race groups as well.

Hester's 'too close for comfort' idea turned on its head for me the idea of self-representation. Hester showed me how psychologically complex it is for people to represent their own groups. With great bravery, she admitted her own difficulties in empathising with white South Africans, especially because she herself was a white South African very critical of apartheid. Hester's story is partly the story of the shame we take on and try to get rid of when thinking about people we see as very like ourselves. If we think back, then, to Tom Shakespeare's useful idea of disabled people being seen as 'dustbins for disavowal' by able-bodied people, we can see, paradoxically enough, that disabled people may be 'dustbins for disavowal' by other disabled people ('I may be disabled, but I'm not like *them*'). I think some of this comes from growing up with all the negative things disabled people have to live with (not all disabled people grow up disabled, but some do). Some of it comes from having repeated experiences of being seen as a representative of a group and not a person in one's own right. Disabled people have to fight to be seen for who they are, to be seen as individuals, and not just as 'the disabled' or 'the representative of the disability movement'. I am, of course, sometimes seen as no more than the representative of a group – as, for example, a white able-bodied man. But because I come from a powerful and very visible group, I am given more chance to be seen as me – I don't have to fight to show that I am quite different from many white able-bodied men, as I am allowed to have an identity apart from just my white able-bodied maleness.

When I think back on my father being less than sympathetic to Ruth lying there in traction, I think I have a better sense now of why that was necessary for him, even though I still believe it was unfair of him. In a similar way, I can't pretend that I see 'Nothing about us without us' as a simple thing, free from all the psychological influences I've been talking about. Would I have it another way? Would I prefer a return to an old system in which do-gooding professionals like me took it upon themselves to speak on behalf of disabled people and to know what is best for them? Never. I believe completely in self-representation. But I do think we need to recognise that no political strategy, no way of counteracting oppression, can itself be free of all the muddle, all the demands and responsibilities, and all the possibility for abuse that other modes of operation carry. And that is part of the richly complex challenge: in solving or meeting certain needs and demands, we move forward but create more challenges. In facing these, we can move forward again.

5

Twisted Feet

After we left Rhodesia in 1966, we lived in small towns close to the cement factories where my father worked. For a few years before my father was transferred to Johannesburg, I was in boarding school in that city, at King David, a Jewish school which prided itself on being progressive and liberal. Sending me to school at King David had not been an easy decision for my father. He would have preferred that I went to Marist Brothers, a single-sex school more similar to the one he had attended. One of his worries was that being at a Jewish school would turn me into a rabbi, which he really didn't want (as they say about being a rabbi, it's not a job for a nice Jewish boy), though he had no worries that Marist, a Catholic school, would turn me into a Catholic priest. In the event, though I flirted a bit with religion while at King David (and going to religious services was helpful in getting me out of early-morning sports practice), if anything the school put me off religion for the rest of my life, but that's another story.

King David was in many ways a wonderful place in the late 1960s and early 1970s. Teachers who could not get jobs in the repressive apartheid state education system came to King David, where there was an atmosphere of possibility and experimentation. My first Jewish history class in high school is particularly memorable. In came Mrs Appelbaum, and her first words to us after general introductions were, 'There were three great prophets in Jewish history. Can you tell me who they were?' We all tried various options but got the answer wrong, until she eventually told us, 'They were Moses, Jesus and Karl Marx.' Quite a history lesson for a Jewish school in apartheid South Africa in 1968. It was also the first time I had ever heard of Karl Marx. Mrs Appelbaum was not alone in her left-wing views. We were taught by people who became well-known left-wing academics and writers in South Africa, trade unionists, and even mad scientists, who, much to our delight, would mix chemicals together incorrectly in the lab and cause explosions.

Nothing in the curriculum was free from this experimental approach. For history in Standard 7, instead of the interminable repetitions of the glories of the Great Trek and the Voortrekkers' covenant with God in return for supremacy over the Zulus, we studied the Vietnam War (still very much ongoing at the time) and even learnt something about the Cuban missile crisis. One of our set books for English was Desmond Morris's *The Naked Ape*, and while our rotund, middle-aged and eminently respectable English teacher looked on, we had to take turns reading from what I now see as Morris's pseudoscientific, implicitly moralistic and prescriptively 'objective' account of how the Naked Ape has sex. This was very titillating to a group of fifteen-year-old boys in the iron grip of South African censorship. Unlike teenagers of today, we had almost no access to pornography and had to work very hard to get to see any dirty pictures at all.

A punctuation exercise in one of our English examinations was taken from a magazine interview with Paul McCartney, at a time when the Beatles were banned from radio in South Africa (there was no television in the country then) because of John Lennon's comment that the Beatles were more popular than Jesus. Our Afrikaans teacher was the wife of an Afrikaner priest who had sided with Beyers Naudé against the apartheid government and had earned the wrath of the authorities, and we were encouraged in all sorts of ways to think about and argue about religion and politics. At that time, Leonard Cohen, the singer-songwriter, was very popular among us students, and we were delighted when his poetry was given to us to analyse alongside the poetry of Shakespeare, Marvell, Milton and Wordsworth. One of the poems we were given to study was 'For Wilf and His House', which begins with the following lines:

> When young the Christians told me
> how we pinned Jesus
> like a lovely butterfly against the wood,
> and I wept beside paintings of Calvary
> at velvet wounds
> and delicate twisted feet.

This was a marvellous poem for young Jewish students to analyse, and I now listen to Cohen with his depressed Canadian voice reading the poem aloud on an MP3 file I have on my computer. For many years after leaving school I remembered the phrases 'lovely butterfly' and 'twisted feet'. As I listen to the poem now, as then at school, I can picture very clearly in my mind's eye the cool white marble of statues of Jesus on the cross at the Roman Catholic schools attended by the children who lived next door to us when we still lived in Salisbury. Bruce, who was my age, was my best friend and he went to St George's; his sisters went to the Convent School. We also used to go with Bruce and his family out to the Chishawasha Mission, not that far from where we lived, to see Brother Waddilove. At the Chishawasha Mission, as at the Catholic schools, there was a statue of Christ on the cross, with his twisted feet.

When I think of the names Chishawasha and Waddilove – evocative names for childhood fantasy characters and places – part of me thinks that they cannot have existed, but when I Google them I find that Chishawasha Mission was established in 1895, and that Brother Waddilove, a Jesuit priest, came to Southern Rhodesia in 1937. In 1963, at the very time we would have visited the mission, he was establishing the first savings club for poor black women in Rhodesia. He believed, I now know, in participation and self-determination for poor and marginalised groups, and in 1967 he contributed to (and probably wrote) the following statement on behalf of Chishawasha Mission:

> The state should not take over work or responsibility from smaller groups when the smaller groups are able to do what is necessary on their own. The reason for this is that if people look to the state for their advancement they fail to acquire the ability to look after their own affairs.[1]

I am amazed to find these things out now. I knew Brother Waddilove, who must have been in his forties at that time, as a vigorous priest stomping around the mission in his dog collar and khaki shorts among the many people who lived and studied there, proudly showing us his vegetables and the sheep and lambs. To me as a child, he was a sort of fantasy figure, but I realise now that at the time I knew him he was espousing principles for marginalised groups that resonate with what I have learnt to be the best of what the disability movement has to offer in terms of its emphasis on local organising and self-determination.

The twisted feet of Jesus in the Leonard Cohen poem, so very Jewish in the way it is written, takes me back, then, from my Jewish high school in Johannesburg to my life as a neighbour of Catholics in Salisbury. Our family did not celebrate Easter and Christmas, but our neighbours did, and I was quite jealous of this. But I was most jealous of two other things about these neighbours. First, they had bacon, which was not allowed in my house, but Bruce used to slip pieces of it to me quite often, much to my gratitude. Second, they had sin. I was fascinated by the concept of sin: it was a sin to do this, a sin to do that, a mortal sin (whatever mortal meant) to do something else. For me there was something racy and dangerously exciting about the idea that there were all these rules and divine punishments, as well as ritualised ways of getting around them through Hail Marys, penances and confessions. The rituals were all so exotic, featuring nuns in habits, priests in cassocks, incense, and statue after statue of Madonna and Child and of Jesus on the cross.

My liberal parents encouraged our finding out as much as we could about other religions and had no objections to our going to church or singing in Carols by Candlelight at Christmas time. (We dealt with the problem of whether this was a betrayal of our beliefs by solemnly agreeing with our Jewish cousins that you are allowed to sing anything you want as long as you don't believe in the Christian bits.) Our Catholic neighbours were similarly tolerant of Judaism (though they must have had their doubts when my mother, of all people, won the first prize of a motor car in the convent raffle). So Bruce and his sisters and my sister and I had ample opportunity to discuss ecumenical and interfaith issues. A lot of this consisted of Bruce and his sisters telling us in no uncertain terms that the Jews killed Jesus, and our protesting that this was ridiculous as Jesus himself had been a Jew. Hence, I suppose, some of the appeal for me of the Leonard Cohen poem – 'When young the Christians told me how we pinned Jesus'. Well, me too.

But for me the appeal of Leonard Cohen went beyond garden-variety Jewish guilt. The image of twisted feet brought to mind not just the lovely marble statues of the crucifixes of my youth. My father had the most twisted feet I knew – his toes were so intertwined that I used to imagine untangling them as one might untangle a knotted shoelace. So the poem about the Jews killing Jesus and pinning him like a lovely butterfly was also a poem about my father and his twisted feet. I remembered this once again when I was doing my internship in clinical psychology at Valkenberg Psychiatric Hospital in Cape Town. A very religious patient came into the ward, reporting that she was bleeding from her hands and her feet, and from her right side. The psychiatrist in charge of the ward, a keen Jungian, excitedly told us about religious stigmata, where patients mimic through their bodies the wounds of Christ on the cross. Though there is a lot of debate in the psychiatry literature about the veracity of reports of stigmata, the issue still attracts considerable interest from cultural psychiatrists and medical anthropologists.[2] I did not have to go far, though, to find someone with stigmata. Not only did my father have twisted feet, he sometimes bled from his side in cold weather. His hands were okay. But this did not stop me from making the connections.

Any psychologist, lawyer or teacher who has worked with children whose parents divorce will know that a large number of these children believe that they are responsible for their parents' marital breakdown. Similarly, when parents suffer any troubles, pain or difficulty, children, and especially young children, may see themselves as the cause of the problem. They may try to make things better for the parents – to be extra good, or to be like parents to their own parents. For as long as I can remember, I thought of my father as powerful (in fact I was quite afraid of his temper), but also broken, sore and harried. I did not need Leonard Cohen or any Christian to tell me how I had 'pinned' my father – been part of something that broke him. I tried in many ways to make things up to him – working very hard at school, for example – but I knew I couldn't do it. Part of me felt (and part of me probably was) even quite cruel to him in my failure to make things better for him, and in my defiant but childlike resistance to becoming what he needed me to be so that he could feel better. I'm not really sure what it was he wanted me to be, but somehow I knew I couldn't do it. As much as it felt like a life-or-death matter that I make things better for my father, I felt that I – the real me – would die if I did this, if I were sub-sumed into this story of family tragedy, authored, it seemed to me, largely by my grandmother. I continue to feel the mixture of trying to make things better and trying equally hard not to make things better, of taking on the blame and refusing to take it on. I still wage this battle with family, with friends and with colleagues, a battle they will recognise between my being supportive and facilitative (empowering, if you like) and feeling overwhelmed by this and just wanting, selfishly, to do something for me me me, as I like to say. I don't blame my father for this, and I wish I could have done things differently, been a better son to him, but there you are. I lived (and live) with a feeling I have in my bones of having let my parents down, of not being what they wanted and needed, even of being a source of shame to them. Some of this, I am sure, comes from a whole lot of things in my family and in myself which have nothing at all to do with my father's impairment, but some of it, for me anyway, links directly to it.

And I don't think I'm all that different in this regard from many children and family members of disabled people. Every child of every parent, every sibling of every other sibling, has fantasies of hurting or causing pain to their loved ones – this is part of what it is to be human. But when that parent or sibling has visible damage already, is in pain or has been hurt, our fantasies about our own power to destroy take on a new meaning. All of us live with our own destructive fantasies, just as we live with our feelings of love and care for others around us; some of us, in fantasy at least, live with the evidence of what destruction is and does – with what we do to cause twisted feet. For me, this is just part of the human condition, but a part which is irrational and not welcomed. All too often we are forced to acknowledge only the positive, character-building sides of being the child or sibling of a disabled person, but we may not want to look at the other sides, which are equally real for many of us.

This way of thinking will not be welcomed by all in the disability field, but I think it's important to acknowledge it. In significant ways we have made such important strides in how we understand disability. We are alert to not falling into the trap of viewing disability as a life (or death) sentence, or of seeing disability as a form of tragedy. We now see disability as we should – as not defining people or their families, as not determining people's lives, as no basis on which to judge what people are like. But when I think about how profoundly my own life has been shaped (not formed, not determined, not limited) by my father's impairments and by the way we as a family dealt with them, I become defiant. We need to redress the balance. It is no shame, and no disgrace to the disability movement or even to the social model, to say that disability matters psychologically, any more than it is shameful to have feelings about anything at all. It is not weakness to speak of these things. It shows, on the contrary, that we have the confidence to recognise that we become strong and empowering, and realise the rights of disabled people and their families, not in spite of our feelings about disability, but partly because of them.

It is no mistake that it is largely through the work of feminist disabled women that we have begun to see how important it is to recognise feelings we have about disability and exclusion, and not to deny these in a misplaced idea that only those who 'overcome' feelings (in a sort of caricature of rough-tough masculinity) can be strong.[3] This is a lesson women have had to teach many freedom or liberation movements. Even in the struggle days in South Africa, it was largely women in the helping professions who made space for thinking about the fact that if we want a good and healthy society we have to take account of the feelings of women, children and men. South Africa, violent society that it currently is, bears testimony to the truth that feelings matter – social exclusion, degradation and the internalisation of shame have consequences for the way people behave towards one another, even in the privacy of their own homes.

But back to me and my time at King David. One of the things I loved about the school was the way in which we were encouraged to find out new things, to search for new information, something that was quite rare in the school system at the time. I even read bits of Freud from books in the school library. For our final school-leaving matric examination we had to prepare orals in Afrikaans and English for inspectors who came to the school and listened to us reading aloud and discussing the material we had chosen. I was fascinated by the Sestigers, a group of experimental Afrikaans writers who prided themselves on their opposition to apartheid. I enjoyed André Brink's novel *Lobola vir die lewe*. For my Afrikaans final oral I read a piece from this book. The author likened the ships of the Dutch settler Jan van Riebeeck entering Table Bay in Cape Town to *'langstert sperme'* (long-tailed sperm). All this was very risqué for a boy my age, but perfect for an Afrikaans oral at King David, home of alternative thinking.

My English oral was more of a challenge to me. I loved Andrew Marvell's 'To His Coy Mistress' (and I still do), and I thought about using that poem for my oral. But this old poem from centuries ago felt a bit too conservative and passé for what we at King David were trying to do. I rooted around in a range of anthologies and eventually came up with Louis MacNeice's poem 'Prayer before Birth', written in 1944. Through the wonders of modern technology and YouTube, it is now possible even to hear MacNeice reading his poem while watching a famous picture of MacNeice's sad, serious face being contorted into shapes approximating how he would have looked had he read the poem on camera. The sound of his voice reading 'Prayer before Birth' is hypnotic and compelling, and I can see many reasons why this poem would have had such appeal to me at the age of sixteen. The poem reads:

I am not yet born; O hear me.
Let not the bloodsucking bat or the rat or the stoat or the
   club-footed ghoul come near me.

I am not yet born; console me.
I fear that the human race may with tall walls wall me,
   with strong drugs dope me, with wise lies lure me,
      on black racks rack me, in blood-baths roll me.

I am not yet born; provide me
With water to dandle me, grass to grow for me, trees to talk
   to me, sky to sing to me, birds and a white light
      in the back of my mind to guide me.

I am not yet born; forgive me
For the sins that in me the world shall commit, my words
   when they speak me, my thoughts when they think me,
      my treason engendered by traitors beyond me,
         my life when they murder by means of my
            hands, my death when they live me.

I am not yet born; rehearse me
In the parts I must play and the cues I must take when

old men lecture me, bureaucrats hector me, mountains
    frown at me, lovers laugh at me, the white
        waves call me to folly and the desert calls
           me to doom and the beggar refuses
             my gift and my children curse me.

I am not yet born; O hear me,
Let not the man who is beast or who thinks he is God
   come near me.

I am not yet born; O fill me
With strength against those who would freeze my
   humanity, would dragoon me into a lethal automaton,
      would make me a cog in a machine, a thing with
         one face, a thing, and against all those
           who would dissipate my entirety, would
             blow me like thistledown hither and
               thither or hither and thither
                 like water held in the
                   hands would spill me.

Let them not make me a stone and let them not spill me.
Otherwise kill me.

My reading of this poem went well in the oral, and though I don't
know what mark I got for the oral itself, I did well in English in
the exams. I remember reading the poem over and over to myself
in the weeks before the oral, as well as reading it to my parents,
who listened indulgently to my various versions. When I look at
the poem now, though, an obvious subtext stands up and hits me
in the face.

My father had twisted toes, as I have described, and in addition his feet were technically described as 'club feet'. According to the National Institutes of Health website, 'Clubfoot is when the foot turns inward and downward. It is a congenital condition, which means it is present at birth.'[4] When I look at the pictures of club feet on the website, though, I see images which look much more innocuous than my memory of my father's club feet even after they were operated on. But what was I, with my club-footed father, doing when I chose for my English oral a poem that refers to 'the club-footed ghoul'? Later in the poem there is another reference about which I feel uncomfortable: 'the man who is beast'. What was I doing reading this poem over and over again to my parents? I had no sense (or no conscious sense) then of the links between my father's club feet and the club feet of the ghoul in MacNeice's poem. It is quite possible that neither of my parents noticed the link either. But I have no doubt at all that something was going on in this choice.

Quite what was going on is more difficult to identify. The first time I made the connection between my choice of the 'club-footed ghoul' poem and my feelings about my father was when I read Mark Raphael Baker's *The Fiftieth Gate*. Baker is an Australian historian and the son of two Jewish Holocaust survivors. The book is a moving blend of memoir and history, and speaks to many things, including the question of who has the right to discuss and own the past. The scene in the book which made the greatest impact on me was Baker's description of dressing up as Hitler for a fancy-dress party when he was a teenager, and his subsequent bemusement at his parents' strong negative reaction to this. My immediate thought on reading this scene was that my 'club-footed ghoul' moment is my equivalent of Baker's 'dressing up as Hitler' moment. And I felt guilty and sore, upset that my father was dead so I could not discuss this with him, but also doubtful that I would have discussed it with him had he lived. My father's death was necessary to my being able to talk about the 'club-footed ghoul' issue, and even to my being able to write this book at all. Who's the ghoul now, you may well ask, club feet or no club feet? Did I, do I, have a club-footed ghoulish heart? And what right do I have to indulge in this self-centred and self-indulgent worrying over my past and my parents when I have had a life so patently less painful, so patently more free, so patently more privileged, than the life led by my disabled father? Not only have I had it better than my father, I have had it better because he was a good man and a good father, and somehow I give myself the right to use him and his life and death to make a book, the writing of which gives me a lot of pleasure.

In an interview about *The Fiftieth Gate*, Baker was asked, 'What prompted you to write a book about your parents?' He replied:

> Well, it's not really about my parents, it's about me growing up with my parents' memories. I teach a course at Melbourne University on the Holocaust. For years, I have been studying everyone else's stories and testimonies. As a teenager, I would read any memoir I could get my hands on. And then suddenly I realised, I'm an historian and yet I know so little about my own history.[5]

I identify with these words of Baker. Just as he is, or was, a historian knowing so little of his own history, I feel that I am, or was, a psychologist knowing so little about my own psychology. But where Baker can say that his book is about his parents' histories, mine is not about the memories of my parents as participants in a ghastly public event, but rather about my making something of my own about our personal lives, and about my father's club-footed body, or body with twisted feet. The appropriation, when I think of it this way, really does feel a bit ghoulish. But still I do it.

And part of why I do it is contained in other reactions that I now have to MacNeice's poem. I love the way MacNeice links beastliness with thinking that one is God, in the line 'Let not the man who is beast or who thinks he is God come near me.' But for MacNeice's poem to work, he needs ghouls and beasts, people who are close to bats, rats and stoats. The language that MacNeice draws on is such familiar language to us all: the ugly, limping witch, the mean little dwarf who stamps his feet, the wicked albino of *The Da Vinci Code*, and so on. No prizes for guessing why, given my family history and my extreme ineptitude at drawing, that the human figures I thought I could draw with the most competence and pleasure when I was a child were ugly witches. But I was making use of a tradition that is entrenched and drawn on by everyone from writers of trashy comic books to the likes of Louis MacNeice – ugly and disabled people are associated with beasts and with evil. It is Rumpelstiltskin who stamps his ugly little foot, and the blond, blue-eyed prince who saves the princess with a kiss.

Even the scientific names we use for impairments tell a story. The technical term for club feet is *talipes equinovarus*. The word *talipes* comes from the Latin words for 'ankle' (*talus*) and 'foot' (*pes*). *Equino* means 'horse-like', and *varus* means 'turned in'. So my father had ankles and feet which were turned in and horse-like. Similarly, the single palm line that we see on the hands of children with Down's syndrome and some other congenital conditions, and which differentiates these hands from those of the rest of us who have two palm lines, is called a 'simian cleft' – *simian* meaning 'like an ape'. A mother of a child with Down's syndrome once said to me, 'I know that my child has one line on her hand, just like an ape, but do they really have to tell me my child is like a monkey?' In some senses, of course they do. This is how we portray disability, even in the supposedly neutral and objective world of science.

There are other, more benign versions of how we look at disability in the media and in our stories. For example, the Hunchback of Notre Dame and the Phantom of the Opera are really gentle souls within their ghastly exteriors. These stories about people who are good and kind despite their looks or disabilities – and, even worse, the myth that is peddled that disabled or ugly people are actually better than or happier than the rest of us – may be well meant. But they reinforce our stereotypes even further. The default position from which they work is that there is some kind of link between physical impairment or disfigurement and morality or happiness. 'Well, I don't know about you,' one may equally say, 'but I've found in general that black people are happy-go-lucky, and that women are naturally kind and gentle.' We all deserve better than this, but it's club-footed ghouls (even club-footed ghouls with hearts of gold) we too often go for.

In the end, in choosing the MacNeice poem for my matric oral, I can't really say what I was doing, or why. It could even be (though I don't buy this) that the club-footed ghoulishness of it was just coincidental – as Freud said, sometimes a cigar is just a cigar. But what I do know without any doubt is that my actions then have meaning for me now. It matters to be the child of a person with twisted feet. It mattered to me, and I don't think I am alone in this. This is not a story of tragedy – my life has been happy, fulfilled and lucky thus far – but a story about recognising things that count, things we should not ignore. I do see club feet and I do see colour. I'm glad I do.

6

I Was a Ninety-Seven-Pound Weakling

My sister is short, but not nearly as short as my paternal grandfather, who died of a heart attack on the golf course before either of us was born. He was, we are told, about five feet tall, and was known in Tarkastad where my father grew up as *'die mooi Joodjie'* (the good-looking little Jew). My sister, like many of the women in the family, has large breasts, and my grandmother's most famous comment to her was, 'Jenny, you are built like your Poor Late Grandfather: very short, and a heavy bosom.' The question arises of how the little Jewish man could be good-looking with his heavy bosom (in an era unliberated in terms of sex and gender, a time about which it was true to say, according to Granny again, 'In my day we never had sex'), but let's just leave it as one of a welter of Grannyisms which have come down through the generations.

My grandmother always favoured me over my sister, and made no apology for this. But though my sister was not one who could 'go on the stage with a handbag' (another Grannyism – don't ask me about the handbag because I don't know), she had a set of talents I definitely did not have. As a young girl she was very good at ballet, and at one time seriously considered continuing with ballet into high school, though her height would have stood in the way of a professional career. For one of her ballet performances all the other girls had to be trees, but Jenny, being too short to be a tree, had a solo part as a leaf. I'm pretty sure now (as we were back then) that the whole idea of having girls dancing as trees and a solitary leaf, instead of dancing as fairies or peasant maidens or whatever, was a ruse on the part of a diplomatic ballet teacher to give Jenny a solo part. Jenny was really good at ballet, whereas for many of the other little girls it was a case of 'Don't put your daughter on the stage, Mrs Worthington.' Jenny had all the talents needed for ballet – she was musical, utterly charming and engaging, free and open with her feelings, and a gifted athlete. In her last year of primary school this little girl who was a head shorter than most of her peers was *victrix ludorum* at the school sports day.

All of this must have been an enormous relief to my mother (and to my father too, I suppose, but it was my mother who spoke of it). Throughout her first pregnancy, and to a lesser extent her later pregnancy (with me), my mother fretted and worried over whether she would produce a disabled child. Nobody had (or has) any idea why my father and his late sister were disabled. My mother's final conclusion, having produced two able-bodied children and now having four able-bodied grandchildren, was that 'Granny must have had funny insides.' I have always simply agreed with this view. My quick scouring of the literature as a layperson throws up a range of speculations for the causes of club feet – including references to chromosomes – but mainly the cause seems to be unknown, with an increased risk in family members. But, as with so much else, we just assume that it's the mother who is somehow the cause.

My father was very proud of Jenny's athletic abilities. In the weeks before school sports days, he would come home from work at the cement factory and help us train for these events. In the beautiful fading light just before the dramatic transition from day to night in Salisbury, he would time our running up and down the gravel road outside our house. The stopwatch he had was magnificent and heavy, and when he wasn't using it he kept it in the box in which he had bought it. I was sometimes allowed to play with it, but carefully and not too much. I don't think Jenny enjoyed these sessions of home-based athletics practice, and she's never really been too keen on sport in spite of her talents, but she ran and ran like the wind, and these were special times with my dad. I can still see my father's creased face smiling at us during these sessions. He was enjoying the simple joy of being out with his children. One of my mother's friends, who I think was always half in love with my father, said she had never under-stood the meaning of the expression 'laughing eyes' until she saw my father's eyes. I feel moved and grateful when I picture my father standing there on the gravel road, stopwatch in hand, dressed in his work clothes of khaki shorts and shirt, long socks, and vel-skoen pushed out of shape by his funny toes, a long shadow behind him, and him squinting slightly into the fading sun and smiling, smiling. There is the smell of the red earth and the bush nearby, and nobody else around, just the three of us – Jenny, Dad and me.

It is moments like these, moments unmarked and unspecial, that are moments of love, moments I think about and cradle to me. These are the times – and I think (I hope) we all have them – which went by almost unnoticed but made so much of what was good about growing up as me. But in spite of the love and longing I feel for these times – and possibly because of the love and longing – things were much more layered than the idyllic late-afternoon scene may imply. I hated running and was bad at it; I was awkward and slow. I was always one of the last in races and I dreaded athletics events. My only achievement on the track was that once – just once – I came third in the egg-and-spoon race, a product of my sheer determination not to drop the egg, and to go as slowly and steadily as I could (a tortoise and hare story). In fact, I was useless at all sports and very poorly coordinated. My father was an excellent sportsman and came from a sporting family, and among my mother's sisters were tennis and bowls champions. Like my mother, though, I was just terrible at sport.

This was a big deal for a boy in the British colony of Southern Rhodesia in the 1960s. Almost nothing, with the possible exceptions of cigarettes and alcohol, was more important to growing into a good and noble Rhodesian man than developing 'character' on the sports field. I learnt every trick in the book to get out of compulsory sports practices. I remember slipping and sliding on the parquet flooring of our passage at home, uncomfortable in my brand-new football boots, and begging and pleading with my mother not to take me to football practice. I was not quite the worst at sports in my class (I usually came second-last in races), but I was still one who, when the two captains took turns to pick sides for rounders, cricket or gymnastics, was left waiting with the very last few – the point at which the captains would say, 'You have him.' 'No, you have him.' Years after my introduction to school sports, I heard Janis Ian's iconic teenage-angst song 'At Seventeen', and some of the lyrics seemed written just for me:

> To those of us who knew the pain
> of valentines that never came
> and those whose names were never called
> when choosing sides for basketball ...

There's not much doubt that whatever else accounted for my difficulties with coordination and sports, I had a genuine physical problem. I remember being taken to a paediatrician in central Salisbury, an elderly man who ran his practice from an old house in the shade of a jacaranda tree. One of the things he asked me to do was to stand on one leg. I did so and promptly fell over. He smiled and asked me to do it again. Again I fell over. He grimaced and asked me to do it once more. I fell over yet again, at which point he blurted out, 'Surely you can stand on one leg for just a few seconds?' As far as I knew I was trying my best, but I could not do what he wanted – I was just too wobbly. Some years later, when I was experiencing knee pain, I went to a physio-therapist who told me accusingly, 'It's not possible that your leg muscles are so weak.' Well, she was looking at them, and they were there in front of her as weak as she saw them. When I had my children, I learnt (and so did they) something about my difficulties with spatial orientation that I had never known before. When they were babies, I would walk around the house carrying them, when, for no reason I could see, they would on occasion start to cry. Before long I realised that each time this happened, I had misjudged door openings in my own home and had scraped my children against walls or door frames. Some people could have a field day with this, talking about my unconscious aggression towards my kids (and of course I have the least authority to talk about my own unconscious), but once I noticed this with my children I began to see that I quite regularly walk into walls and door frames and right myself without even noting this as unusual.

There were other signs of my spatial problems. I did well at school right from the beginning, but would get into trouble for some things. In my first year of school, one of the activities we had to do for the hapless Miss van der Riet, who was absent more than she was present, or so it seemed to me (boyfriend problems, I suspect), was to roll pieces of plasticine into long sausages and then shape each piece into the number '2' and put them in rows on a piece of hardboard. This was probably an exercise based on the modern educational ideas of the time – that children learn best by doing, and in the tactile mode. I, who could already do sums in my head with numbers as big as ten, dutifully made my twos. All of them except one were back to front, and Miss van der Riet was very unhappy with this. In a further attempt at progressive teaching, she gave us little picture sums to do. For example, there would be three little houses, a plus sign, another little house, and then an equals sign. All we had to do was to produce four little houses to the right of the equals sign. I just couldn't do it, though I had no trouble at all with $3 + 1 = 4$ if it was given to me in figures. This inconsistency made Miss van der Riet even more exasperated and angry, and probably contributed to her taking more days off, when we could blissfully visit Mrs Simms' class. Mrs Simms was older, fatter, more experienced and altogether better cut out for junior-grade teaching. She was also far more indulgent of my shocking handwriting.

I don't have any doubt that these strange anomalies in the way I learnt at school, as well as my inability to balance, to catch a ball and to orientate myself properly in space, were linked in such a way that today an occupational therapist would have been able to help me. I would have been one of the many beneficiaries of the contemporary poor-muscle-tone, eye–hand-coordination, neuro-developmental training industry, and I've no doubt that it would have done me the world of good. But I think there was something more to my difficulties. One part, I suppose, was that academic things came very easily to me, and I quickly learnt that there were areas in which I could excel and which I enjoyed very much – everything else (like playing cricket) was just too difficult, so I could not be bothered to keep trying, or could not bear not to be the best. But this does not explain my anguish about sports and games when I was little – I was desperately worried about my pitiful performance in this area. Another story will shed some further light on this huge issue for me growing up.

When I was ten years old we left Salisbury, where I had managed to worm my way out of school sports quite successfully and with minimal sanction from a school with a progressive, kind and indulgent headmaster. My next school was Lichtenburg Primary, a small school in a rural town which remains part of the heartland of the white right wing in South Africa. Mothers (well, white mothers, anyway) didn't have much to entertain themselves with other than the achievements of their offspring, and for the first time I was exposed to a group of very competitive mothers who took school sports very seriously. Apart from school sports and various fêtes at which they sold toffee apples and the like, these mothers didn't, as the saying goes, get out much, and this was long before the age of television in South Africa and before aerobics, 'me time' and finding your inner spiritual being. School swimming galas, which had not been a big deal in Salisbury, were huge events in Lichtenburg, and mothers crowded round the newly built school pool (the product of hundreds of cake sales and bring-and-buys) to cheer their children on and to show off their offspring's prowess to one another. This was serious business, make no mistake, and probably part of what kept the white man where he belonged – in power and on top.

Much to my horror, taking part in school sports was compulsory, and I had to participate in at least one race in the gala. Though I loved being in the swimming pool to play about, I was predictably a terrible swimmer, though not quite as bad a swimmer as I was a runner or cricketer. I had taken a long time to learn to swim, had a dreadful swimming style and was slow. My 'best' stroke (the only one I could do vaguely passably) was breaststroke, and I was duly entered in the under-eleven boys' one-length breaststroke race. At that time I was short for my age and very thin, and I couldn't dive as the other boys could. I shivered on the side of the pool – I was in the extreme left-hand lane – and when the whistle went I jumped in and just swam and swam, wanting the ordeal to be over as quickly as possible. I got a few kicks and head- and elbow-butts along the way, adding to my agony. When I reached the wall, I discovered to my amazement that I had arrived not at the deep end of the pool in my own lane, but close to the deep end at the opposite wall of the pool. I had started off in the left-hand lane, had swum diagonally across the pool and was now in the extreme right-hand lane, close to, but not at, the deep end. This explained the kicks and buttings I had received: I had crashed into almost every other boy in the race on my relentless (but skew) push to get the wretched race over. What greeted me when I exited the pool was the unforgettable sight of a range of Lichtenburg mums in various states of distress and disarray, some in tears, some berating my mother for the terrible sin I had committed. What I had done was to cut across the paths of all other swimmers and to ruin the chances their darlings had of bettering their times in the race. This was, I realise in retrospect, my crowning moment in sport – more magnificent even than coming third in the egg-and-spoon race. Single-handedly I had shattered the legitimate and noble sporting aspirations of a group of ten-year-old boys and their mothers, mothers who had given all for the good of the country and the white race.

I tell this story with a chest that swells with pride, a pride all the greater because the nobility I had shown in playing dirty on the sports field (all right, sports pool) was all the greater as this nobility was completely unintentional. It came from a place so instinctual, so much part of me, that my great manliness was at last shown. I realised none of this at the time, but where sport is concerned I must take my due spoils, however delayed they may be. But another thing I did not realise at the time relates to the obvious mathematics of what happened in the pool that fateful day. I had swum along the hypotenuse of a triangle the sides of which were the width from left to right (the shorter of the two right-angled sides), and almost the entire length of the pool (the longer of the right-angled sides). By Pythagoras, I had swum further than the other boys, all of whom swam straight. But if I crashed into them one by one, I must have swum faster than at least some of them in order to reach them as they dashed along in the right direction. Only a swimmer not quite as slow as I had thought I was could have done this. There are many morals to this story (some more hilarious than others), but the one that is most important for my purpose here is that my complete conviction about my athletic uselessness might have been, in swimming at least, misplaced to some degree.

Now I am neither the first nor the last person to underestimate his athletic skill. But what interests me is the ferocity with which I hung on to my sporting incompetence. I was not just a person who had difficulty doing things like running and catching a ball. For as long as I can remember, these difficulties have been part of my core identity, an identity I have fiercely asserted. Despite the fact that I am quite physically fit now, especially for a man of my age, I hang on to my non-athleticism with a vehemence and defiance which suggest that there is more at stake than my physical shortcomings. I am sometimes stubborn, and that is part of it, but not all of it.

Some of it may have to do with my mother. There's no question that she worried about whether my sister and I would be okay physically even before (especially before) we were born. As an infant I did not feed well, and my mother recounts a famous scene in which an irascible paediatrician said to my mother, who was worried about my health, 'The child's malnourished – get him on good formula feeding immediately!' I remained a painfully thin child (this continued until adulthood, and as I now battle to keep my weight down I ruefully long for the days of being too thin!). My mother was ashamed of this, I think. I loved swimming at the communal pool near the cement factory, but my mother would not let me wear the little Speedo bathing costumes all the other boys wore. Because I was so thin, she insisted that I wear swimming trunks high enough to cover my belly button. This, of course, made me stand out even more, and was so out of keeping with the rest of the way I was brought up, which was down-the-line liberal Dr Spock. But even though I can see that this worry on the part of my mother could have been one (even a key) contributor to my insistently non-athletic identity, it feels to me that there was something more, and more fundamental, going on.

My father, like all fathers, had wishes and hopes for me, and among those, I'm sure, were hopes for what I'd do on the sports field. This is not that unusual, of course. Part of my crazy envy of my nephew Adam when he was a baby in the Babygro my father called his 'Parkhurst Rovers' outfit was at seeing my father's wish for a sporting son transferred to this more likely candidate. As it happens, both Adam and his brother Dean did become good sportsmen and soccer players, and it's sad that my father did not live to see this. Part of what I experienced from my father, though, was a more urgent wish than that experienced by sons of other fathers. My father wanted me to enjoy and be good at sport, not just to continue a family tradition of masculinity, but also so I could do things he couldn't do. He had not been able to play rugby, for example, which was a huge issue for a boy at his colonial school in the 1930s. He wanted me to have the joy of sport, but in some sense he also wanted me to play sport on his behalf. This seems to me the most natural and unexceptionable wish in the world: we all have wishes for our children, and we all hope that they will not experience the pain and difficulties that we have experienced.

I can't imagine what it must have been like for my father, after the relief of finding that I was not disabled as he was, to realise that I had no natural aptitude for sports. How must it have been for him that I walked only at eighteen months? He must have been proud that I talked so early, and I have often been told that people found it very cute that I could recite nursery rhymes while I was still crawling. Every parent who has a child who walks very late must have some anxiety, but there must have been an extra worry for my father that, like him, I would not walk properly. But then I did walk and all was well. Perhaps I could still be a sportsman. But I was clumsy, and did not enjoy physical things much. Nowadays we have words for this sort of behaviour, useful words in the lexicon of occupational therapy, words which can help us remediate the kind of problems I had. But the words available in Rhodesia of the 1950s and 1960s, the Rhodesia of the newly established housing estate and cement factory, were words like 'lazy', 'naughty' and 'sissy'. My father was never unkind to me about my lack of prowess, and he never called me names (nor would he have tolerated this from others). But to expect him not to have been affected by all of this would be to expect him to have been superhuman. From very early on, then, battle lines, lines that neither of us had ourselves drawn up, were drawn between me and him. He wanted me to be something for him and for myself; some parts of what he wanted I just couldn't do. And early on, I think, I decided that if there were things I couldn't do for him, the way I could get back in control in this battle over my body, the way for me to survive, and to win, was to decide that I wouldn't do things for him. Compromise for me was no option at all, because it felt like capitulating in a grand story in which I could only lose. I could not just be the kid who's bad at sport but enjoys taking part. I had to go the whole hog and hate the lot.

I can go on and on about the possible additional layers of this. For example, I have little doubt that my father felt some anger towards me for being so useless at something so important to him, but sensitive man that he was, and mindful of his own experiences with his own loudly disappointed mother, he held back his disappointment and anger towards me. So I took on the task of punishing myself and my own body, partly on his behalf. There was also the difficult issue of my own unbroken body versus his broken one. Could it be that I could not allow myself the pleasure of physical exercise because this would in some ways show up his body as more broken than mine? If I held back physically, I did not have to deal with the issue of my having triumphed, in a way, over his broken and hurt body. I'm sure there are other things I haven't even considered here, other possibilities, but for me a key reality of my life is that the way I feel about my body, in my body, for my body, is in some ways a product of my father's being disabled. It is not about my father having been a bad parent, or worse than any other parents, on the basis of his disability – far from it. I know that the talents I have and the joy I feel in life come from him too. It is about the fact that, like it or not, disability matters, and can matter fundamentally.

My determination to be almost anti-physical was somehow a necessity for me, but it was costly. I used to fantasise about being able to give my body to somebody else who had been hurt in a car crash and to continue living in a much reduced physical state – as a sort of mind without a body. I had no sense of what this might mean, and even I, sitting as I am now typing this, find it hard to credit such a fantasy, because I enjoy so much about physical life, about having a body. But from a very young age I forced my physical ineptitude, my lack of interest in sports, my wimpishness, in other people's faces. I was not going to allow these things to be incidental when they felt so central to me. I was aggressive in my own apparently weak way: 'This is who I am,' I was saying. 'Take me or leave me.' This gave me some control over what was most difficult for me, and I never begged, pleaded or compromised. When I was a teenager, my sister Jenny suggested that for my father's sake I should pretend to be interested in sport even if I did not play sport. Would this have been so terrible? Not at all. But my way was the way that was most controlling, and most cruel for both my father and me. He had to accept that I was different from him, that there was a way in which I had let him down; otherwise, no deal. That was the basis on which I could be his son, and there was no room for argument.

I hang my head in shame. How could I have been so cruel? I had no sense of my cruelty, certainly, and I thought for a long time that I was simply a victim in this. But I now see that part of my being so determinedly physically weak was the best way I could punish my father for being disabled, for not having the body other boys' fathers had. We both paid for this. In the end, it may not be so terribly important, but I do regret it, and I wish I could have discussed this with my father.

I can say that things have got much better. When I was twenty-four, I began my professional training in clinical psychology. My choice of career was not an obvious one for a clever Jewish boy who was good at maths. More than half of the people in my high-school class did medicine, but this never really felt like an option for me after years of hearing my father being berated for not being a doctor. My father was keen for me to be an actuary because I was good at maths, but somehow my rebelliousness mixed in with good sense and I did a combined arts and science degree and then continued with psychology. I was happy (am happy) with clinical psychology as a career choice. As part of the requirements for the course, and also because I wanted to do this, I went into therapy with a kind and supportive psychotherapist. This was also a very good experience for me. Added to all of this, I was in love. All these good things together conspired against my hatred of my own body, and soon I was swimming at the university swimming pool every day. I have little recollection of the first time I went to the pool, but I do remember feeling self-conscious. I could not swim a full length of an ordinary-sized pool. But by the end of that year I was swimming a mile a day.

Over the years, I have been better and worse about getting exercise, like many middle-aged, middle-class people with busy lives. The past two years have been especially good – I go to gym regularly. I struggle with the gym as a public space in which the body is so valorised. I feel self-conscious, and I don't try out new exercises easily. But I do it. And while I am at gym, I find myself often feeling grateful for the fact that I can exercise with no pain, and thinking about my dad and his funny sore body, smiling in the fading light on the road outside our house. I put us both through hell and I'm sorry for that. But I'm grateful too. We do what we need to do.

7

Bride of Frankenstein

Auntie Tilly had a wonderful turn of phrase. Her idea of a balanced meal was 'an ice-cream cone in each hand', and she was known to practise what she preached. She called people who were aggressive 'punchy', as in 'She's much too punchy for her own good, that one,' and she was not above suggesting in their absence that people who talked too much nonsense should 'take a *shtum* powder'. In the early 1970s she delighted in saying that 'we are a hippy family', and she was right. She had hip problems, and so did my father, Auntie Ada, Dinky and Ruth. Inadvertently, I have carried on the family tradition.

I was introduced to the love of my life by a friend, at what was a very difficult time for me. I was depressed and miserable, and Kerry said to me, 'You have to meet Louise – she's such a nice person. She also likes going to gym, and she also likes reading books.' There were lots of other things we had in common. We were both psychologists and had similar political views, and in fact we have worked out that we must have met years earlier at a sociology conference in Stellenbosch. At that time we were both happily involved with other people, and we took little notice of each other at a large table under the oaks, accompanied as we were by friends and colleagues we had in common. I also had no idea at that time that this foreign country of Stellenbosch would one day become a treasured work home for me, and central to both our lives.

I was not much one for going on 'dates', but I agreed to meet Louise briefly before going off on holiday – she was visiting Kerry in Cape Town. I was immediately smitten, as they say (it's hard not to use clichés for love), and my subsequent life with Louise has been a blessing and a joy. But here's the thing: I had already fallen in love with Louise (I fell, as they say further, hard and fast) when I found out that she had, of all things, a congenital hip problem. Now if this isn't an opportunity for a Freudian smug fest I don't know what is – it doesn't take a great deal of intelligence or insight to make some sort of interpretation about my marrying what I am used to, or trying to right some sad childhood wrong through repairing things in this relationship. What intrigues me about my choice of Louise as a partner is that I fell for her before I knew about the hip, and that when I learnt about the hip it was just one of those things. I have no problem at all with the idea that indeed I was attracted to something familiar, something I could try to make better for myself in the second half of my life. But how did I know? What did I see? Or was it all coincidence after all? I don't know. I also know that it is not possible to reduce my choice to one determined only by Louise's impairment – she is much more than her bad hip, as the social model would emphasise. What's more, though her hip problem would suggest that Louise is more broken than I am, in many important ways this feels untrue. She is probably the bravest, most fearless person emotionally that I have ever met, much stronger in this respect, it feels, than I am. But in the end it's not a competition between us to see who's stronger and who's weaker. I think we can support each other and help each other in life, and that's what it's about, for me anyway.

It was only after I met and fell in love with Louise that I began to think more about my mother's choice to marry my father. There are obvious parallels between her choice and mine: we both chose to marry someone with physical impairments, though Louise's impairments are less obvious than those of my father. But where I may just be modelling my behaviour on that of my poor old mum (and there are worse things to do), what was my poor old mum doing? When I discuss this with her, her answer is quite simple. She fell in love with my father as a whole person, and his hip and his funny feet and his limp were really not the issue. And having grown up with my parents as my parents, I know from the inside how my father's physical problems were not at the centre of their relationship. They talked, talked, argued, talked – it is this I think about more than anything else when I think of them. They were affectionate with each other and they loved each other and they talked all the time.

I can with no effort at all make up another story about my mother, just as I can make up another one about myself. In this story we have the unwanted youngest daughter of a couple with too many children already, with a disabled eldest sister who caused great anxiety to her parents. This youngest daughter had low self-esteem and chose to marry a disabled man in order to repair her own losses and difficulties she experienced as a child. QED. There may be elements in this story that are true, but the story is so crude and generalising that they could be true for almost anybody. And the story demeans my mother and the complexity of her choices in life. Just as the story of Son of Disabled Man With Bad Hip Chooses To Marry Woman With Bad Hip So He Can Repair Broken Childhood tells me something about me, but it also demeans me, turns me into someone less than I am. The problem with these stories is not that they are false but that they are, as the witches in *Macbeth* said, 'honest trifles'. They are part of the truth masquerading as the whole truth.

It's fair to say that psychoanalysis at its worst, and its popularisation, is at least partly responsible for this sort of masquerading. Though psychoanalysis at its best and truest is about doubt, about not knowing, about never knowing the whole truth about anything or anyone, all too often it has become just the opposite. In some of the popularisation of psychoanalysis of the 1940s in particular, but still in some of the worse forms today, there is a kind of know-it-all cleverness by which people claim authority over other people and over society as a whole. Armed with the unique insights of psychoanalysis, we can see the truth about others, even when they can't see these truths themselves. Adding a pseudoscientific spin to the homily 'There are none so blind as those who will not see', psychoanalysis at its worst blames people with any physical impairment for that impairment. Extrapolating from the useful insight that some aspects of emotion may be felt physically – that there really do appear to be, for example, things like psychogenic blindness or seizures of emotional origin – we begin to make the mistake of blaming people for their own impairments and illnesses. Thankfully, this kind of thinking is in decline, but it has been revived in endless women's magazine articles, holistic healing tracts and self-improvement guides. Google the words 'I beat cancer' or 'They told me I would never walk again', and you will find hit after hit, of varying quality, but many of them saying essentially the same thing: through the power of the Human Spirit, or God, or Inner Strength or similar good things, it is possible to overcome terminal illness or disability. Motivational speakers have built careers on catchy phrases like 'They told me I would never walk again ... so I learnt to run.'[1] I am all for inspirational experiences and I think many of these articles and workshops do a lot of good, both for those who write them and for those who read them. But there is a nastily moralistic side to all of this.

If it is the case that people who are especially strong emotionally, who really visualise their recovery well, who are spiritually very advanced, can be 'cured' of illness and disability, what does this say about the millions who don't get cured? Are they just not strong enough emotionally, not spiritual enough, not good visualisers? The moral language about taking responsibility for health and happiness has the useful side benefit of allowing us not to feel bad about blaming people for their impairments or misfortunes. And if we don't want to be so crude as to blame disabled people for their own disabilities, one thing we can now do, with impunity, is to blame those who choose to love disabled people. This is going to take some explaining, but let me try.

First, we need to go back to thinking about how disability is seen in general. Disability activism and scholarship has done us all a great service by showing us how stereotypes inform how we have traditionally looked at disability. As Kathleen McDougall and her colleagues have suggested, it's possible to look at images of disability in historical perspective.[2] Paradoxically, probably the most important image of disability is no image at all – disability is just ignored or hidden away, and there is also a tradition of linking disability with being locked away, imprisoned, confined. In the preface to their celebrated volume on nineteenth-century women writers, Sandra Gilbert and Susan Gubar note that at the centre of much nineteenth-century writing by women were

> images of enclosure and escape, fantasies in which maddened doubles functioned as asocial surrogates for docile selves, metaphors of physical discomfort manifested in frozen land-scapes and fiery interiors – such patterns recurred throughout this tradition, along with obsessive depictions of diseases like anorexia, agoraphobia, and claustrophobia.[3]

These are powerful words, and words that ring true. Disabled and mad people have indeed been portrayed as locked away, and as physical manifestations of the consequences of all sorts of oppression, misuse of power, unhappiness and rage.

A related development in how we perceive disability is to view it as monstrous, evil or a punishment. This is where club-footed ghouls come in, and their surrogates, such as the monster created through human arrogance in Mary Shelley's *Frankenstein*. Disability may also be seen as a tragedy, a terrible curse, or a gift from God for people strong enough to deal with disability. More recently, we have seen the 'supercrip' phenomenon, the portrayal of some disabled people as superheroes, overcoming enormous obstacles to triumph over adversity in spectacular ways: 'Men Climb Kilimanjaro in Wheelchairs';[4] 'Touch the Top of the

World: A Blind Man's Journey to Climb Farther than the Eye Can See';[5] 'Beating the Odds: Beauty Queen with Cerebral Palsy'.[6] A number of comic book superheroes are disabled, such as Daredevil, who is blind but able to use a special 'sixth sense'.

What do all these images of disability say about people who fall in love with disabled people, people who choose to spend their lives intimately involved with disabled people? When disability is seen as a tragedy, we may ascribe nobility to anybody who chooses to be a partner to a disabled person – the woman (and it's usually a woman in the way we imagine these things) who sacrifices her own life to nurture the genius, the talent, the inner humanness of the tragically disabled man. On the surface this may look like a good thing, a celebration of caring, but it is also insulting. Apart from the way in which this image perpetuates and expands gender stereotypes, it creates a demeaning image of a relationship, in which one partner gives everything and there is little mutuality. The power of the carer/partner is accessed only indirectly – through doing good works or through ensuring that the power of the disabled person is realised.

The club-footed ghoulish image of disability presents us with similar stereotypes. As we can see from films like *King Kong*, the image of a kind of raw, naked masculinity combined with a lack of understanding and a vulnerability are portrayed as sexually attractive. We can look at women in relation to disabled men as either taming their beastliness and turning it into something acceptably sexual, or drawing out their manliness from a broken shell, liberating their true maleness. And with supercrips (most of whom are men), women return to the docile role.

What strikes me as I think about these things is how little we have in the way of stereotypes for men who become romantically involved with disabled women. Of course it's not really surprising that this is so – when we think about gender stereotypes, why would a red-blooded man want anything other than a complete woman? I write these words with irony, but still they disgust me because they speak to so many layers of discrimination against disabled people. But when we do think about men who marry disabled women, one of the images that comes to mind is that of abuse. There's no question that there are men who marry and abuse disabled women, that disabled women are more likely than other women to be abused in a host of ways, including sexually. But for me there's something very disturbing when a cultural stereotype we bring to mind when thinking about the relation-ship between an able-bodied man and a disabled woman is that of abuse. What does this say about what we think about disability and sexuality?

To make matters worse, as it has become less socially accept-able to stigmatise disabled people, to blame disabled people for their impairments, we can easily engage in the game of stigma by association. Here's the simple pseudo-psychoanalytic truism: people who fall in love with disabled people do so because they are nuts. Only people who have huge emotional difficulties would get involved romantically with disabled people – 'normal' people, of course, choose 'normal' partners. My friend Valerie Sinason's retort to this would be, as she often says, 'All marriages are made in heaven and in hell.' That is, we all find partners, disabled and not disabled, for the best and the worst reasons. This is life, and the fact will be familiar to anyone who has ever been in a relationship long enough to get past the initial honeymoon stage. But when one partner is disabled, it's so easy to think that we know about the motives and, indeed, the psychopathology of the able-bodied partner. And I'm ashamed to say I've been guilty of this myself. Many years ago I met a very unattractive woman with low self-esteem who had chosen to marry a blind man. Quick as a flash, I made in my mind the cruel interpretation that she'd chosen this man because she knew he'd never know how ugly she was. In my own defence, I'm willing to concede that it's quite possible that this might have been a factor in her choice, but I had (and have) no basis on which to draw these sorts of conclusions. Had she married a sighted man, there would also have been good and bad reasons for her choice, but I would not have been jumping to conclusions. Another friend managed to stigmatise both partners simultaneously. 'Well,' he said, 'this is just a perfect match. She would never have got a sighted man to marry her because she's so ugly, so she's lucky to get a husband, and he's lucky to have found such a nice person who will look after him so well.' All very kind and well-meaning, but so insulting to both partners.

The gay disabled writer, comedian and filmmaker Greg Walloch has a wonderful scene at the centre of his film *F**k the Disabled*. He has reproduced the text of this scene in a book, and it's worth quoting it in full here:

> I was sitting at brunch with a friend of mine. She said, 'Greg, can I ask you a personal question?' and I said, 'Sure,' because you know, I'm very open that way. She said, 'Is the reason that you're gay due to the fact that you're crippled and you can't get lucky with women, so you had no other choice but to sleep with men for sex? You know, I was just wondering.'

I looked at her and was like: 'Are you reading my mind? I was just thinking about that! Yes, that is exactly the reason I sleep with men, it's a sad story, my life. You see, underneath it all I'm actually a heterosexual man, but because of my unfortunate, grotesque disfigurement I was shunned by women and polite society and forced into the depravity of the underground world of man-to-man sex. I never much cared for sucking dick, but if I wanted any action I had better get used to it ... and all the while, in my chest beat the heart of a broken man.'

My friend's like: 'That's nice, Greg. Can you pass the butter?'

I explained to her that it was a matter of economics and weighing my options at the time. Should I waste my money on expensive female prostitutes or be gay? Instead of spending my money on expensive hookers, I found I could get free sex from gay men who had a discriminating eye for fashion, but not for sexual partners. I decided that being gay was cheaper, but I had no idea about hidden costs: the parades, the clothes, the expensive party drugs ... not to mention the apartment in Chelsea, a pretty daunting political agenda, and the painful anal shenanigans. Ouch!

I never wanted to be gay. I tried to fight it, but soon I found I'd developed a strange addiction to crack ... a different kind of crack. You know, the sacrifices that the disabled have to make in this country today because of lack of acceptance are unbelievable! If you're disabled, don't make the same mistakes I did; don't let this happen to you.

That's why I started my own foundation called 'Fuck the

Disabled.' So if you're a woman eighteen to thirty-five and you would like to 'Fuck the Disabled,' call us at 212-DIS-ABLE.

Are you attracted to subservient men? Well, crippled guys can barely stand up. Have you had bizarre sexual fantasies involving a midget or several midgets? We can help. And you know what they say about mentally retarded men? Small intellect, big ... you know what I'm talking about.

So call us: 212-DIS-ABLE. Fuck the Disabled to keep the disabled from turning gay.[7]

I really like this scene in Walloch's film, partly because it is so funny, but also because he manages to encapsulate so much about our prejudices about disability and sexuality. He forces us to re-think everything we hold to be true about disabled people, their sexuality, and the people who have sex with and love disabled people. It's not just perverted fetishism which draws people together. It's a huge range of things, both good and bad, which make such relationships happen – and some of them work and some of them don't.

But does the fact of one person having an impairment have consequences for the relationship? Does it matter? I think it does, and I think it would be as dishonest to say it doesn't as to say that people fall in love just because of the impairment. When I first met Louise, she was physically active (she swam regularly), and looked young and fit. My mother's first impression of Louise was very positive but she was worried. 'Isn't she a little young for you, dear?' my mother wanted to know. Given that Louise is only eighteen months younger than me, I didn't think so!

Although Louise was fit and looked after her health, she knew that because of her congenital hip displacement and subsequent arthritis, she was getting to the point where she would need to have a hip replacement. The pain and deterioration of the hip were becoming too great, and all the orthopaedic surgeons we saw recommended surgery. The year Louise came down from Johannesburg to live with me in Cape Town was the year of her hip replacement, as it turned out, and this was a major event in the lives of the whole family. We were looking forward to the operation, as we'd been told that the procedure has wonderful results, especially in younger patients like Louise.

The day before the operation Louise swam her usual kilometre in the pool, and we talked into the night about all the walks we would take in the Cape Peninsula when Louise was well and at last able to hike after years of pain. I was so grateful she'd come to live with me and my family and I wanted to share with her my love of the Cape. An added bonus was that her hospital room had a beautiful view of the mountain, which seemed meant just for us.

We were told by the surgeon that the operation would be quite routine and should take about two hours. After Louise had been in theatre for about three hours, her parents (who had come down to be with her for the operation) and I were told that there was nothing to worry about, but the operation would take another few hours and we should go have some tea. I took Louise's parents for tea at a restaurant, and I can still see my half-eaten slice of cheesecake sitting on the plate, its pale-yellow crumbs mixing with the icing-sugar garnish. David and Rose told me something of what it had been like for them to have had a sick baby like Louise (she spent most of her first few years in hospital), and about their anguish that for a long time after she came out of hospital, if she saw street lights from the car, she would become distressed as they reminded her of the lights in the operating theatres where she had undergone so many operations. We could hardly bear to be away from the hospital, and we were at tea for no more than half an hour, but in that very short time I felt that something had happened to bind me more closely to Louise's family. What they were talking about in terms of her childhood made me feel sad for all of them, but at the same time I could recognise in their story parts of my own story, and the story of my father, and the story of Dinky's daughter Ruth.

Louise's operation took about six hours in total. Finally the exhausted surgeon came to tell us that there had been a lot of scarring and adhesions from the childhood surgeries which had made this procedure difficult. He was pleased with the result of the operation, though, and said it was a success. In Louise's ward was a woman in her seventies who had had a hip replacement the day before and she was already walking around on crutches, commenting on the miracle that now, only a day after the surgery, her excruciating hip pain of the past ten years had disappeared. This immediate relief, we had been told, was quite common, and it lasted. We were very hopeful for the same results for Louise.

But Louise did not experience immediate relief. She was in agony. She did everything she was told, and within a few weeks of the operation she was even back in the swimming pool (just walking a few steps), on the instructions of the post-operative physiotherapist. Yet the pain continued unabated. Although she was never one to complain, Louise phoned the surgeon to ask what she should do. When she told him she had pain, the doctor's response was, 'That's very unlikely.' Six weeks after the operation, with Louise in severe pain, we went to see her surgeon for a post-operative check-up. He looked at the X-rays, examined Louise, and with great satisfaction told us the operation had been a success. After a five-minute consultation, he was waiting for us to leave when I said, 'But Louise is experiencing a lot of pain. Is there something we can do?' Without looking at Louise or asking her anything at all, he said to me, 'You know, when they're intelligent and when they're young, they tend to complain a lot of pain.'

In retrospect I can't fathom why we kept on going to this doctor. It was clear even then that, good surgeon though he was (and I have no doubt of this), it was more important for him to maintain his belief in his ability to eradicate pain than to deal with a rare case in which he had not succeeded. Louise communicated with him assertively, telling him after a few months, 'Look, I'm a psychologist and I know about psychogenic pain. I know it's possible to feel pain for no organic reason. And I've had enough therapy to know that this is not one of those times. There's something wrong here.' But her doctor, who I am sure in many ways is a very kind man and wants the best for his patients, could not and would not hear any of this. He couldn't bear it that Louise was in pain, and therefore there was no way she could be in pain. That was that.

Eventually we went to another surgeon. He looked at her X-rays and then said, 'There's a particular point where I think you will be most sore.' He pressed this point with his thumb, and Louise felt extreme pain. He had hit the point, visible on the X-rays, where Louise had bone rubbing roughly on bone. More

My grandparents' engagement photograph:
George Swartz and Marlie Wulfsohn, c. 1915.
My grandmother was always a bit unclear
about when she got engaged, but it was
some time around her eighteenth birthday

My father with Sister Stowe,
who looked after him as an infant, 1921

My father as a toddler, 1923.
Note the small walking stick

Auntie Lea and my father, 1936, captured
by one of those street photographers now
long gone. As you can see, Auntie Lea was
stylish but not pleasant

My father after his major operation in England, 1939, just before war broke out

My father. The inscription reads: *To Mum and Dad love Alfred 16/9/48*

My parents on their wedding day, 1951. My mother always protests that she was not a beautiful bride in her borrowed wedding dress, but pictures tell their own stories

My grandmother, my father and my mother, early 1950s. This threesome was the story of my mother's married life

My father and grandfather, *'die mooi Joodjie'*, shortly before my grandfather died, 1951

My mother and Jenny and me aged a few months, 1956. Not the most auspicious debut

My father and Jenny and a friend, 1954. My father is in his typical work clothes

My parents in 1956, shortly after moving to Salisbury.
This is probably my favourite picture of them together

Jenny and my father, 1958. He loved seaside holidays
and always had time for us on such occasions

Jenny and me on the beach. My mother believed in big sun hats before they were fashionable and, though grateful now, I was mortified then

My father at Scottburgh, 1961. He was never afraid of showing his unusually shaped chest and his club feet

On the beach at Scottburgh, 1961. This photograph was taken just before a huge flood which hemmed us in for days

Auntie Lea (left), Granny (second left), and their eldest sister Auntie Mary (second right) with their cousins, 1966. As I read the picture, not a happy gathering

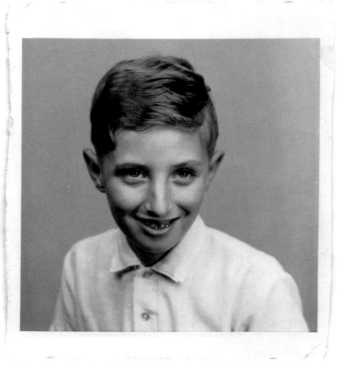

This was taken shortly after I had braces fitted at the age of eleven. People who see it now say I look angelic; I just remember the pain!

Four generations: my grandmother, my father, Jenny and Adam, 1980

My father in 1982, shortly before he died.
To my eyes, he aged well, and kindly

The dilapidated house at White's, 2006 –
a grand folly that is no more

Disability training meeting in Botswana, 2008. This was the first of a series of research training meetings, which continue at the time of writing. This is work I enjoy and feel most drawn to

Clockwise from top left: Me, Rebecca, Louise and Alison, 2009.
An utterly conventional photograph of an unusual group of people

important than the evidence we now had of there being some-thing physical there after all (something we'd never doubted) was the relief we felt that at last Louise was being listened to. The new surgeon made no promises of relief, explaining that the pain was primarily a result of a rare complication of hip-replacement surgery being done in a particular style. The top of the femur had not knitted together and nothing could be done about this, the primary source of the problem, but he could do some rescue surgery to remove some of the hardware that was also causing Louise pain. This second operation helped a great deal, but, as the new surgeon said, the challenge now was for Louise to live with pain, and pain which was patterned very differently from anyone else's.

For example, for reasons nobody can quite understand, Louise can't swim any more – this leads to very bad pain for a long time. She's tried every style possible, she's been to biokineticists and physiotherapists, and swimming just never works. For about nine years after the hip replacement, there was hardly any improve-ment in pain levels. Over the past year or so things have got better, partly because of the efforts of an exceptionally good physio-therapist. Louise deals with pain and with the sleep disturbance that pain causes with an equanimity which I find remarkable – I would be permanently irritable if I were in her position.

Our relationship is not and has never been only about the pain, but the pain has affected how we are together in all sorts of ways. I have learnt to read Louise's face and body movements very closely and carefully, and I can often tell whether she is in pain just by looking at her face in repose. There is lots we can't do together and we still feel wistful about all the forest walks we had planned which will never happen. The pain affected what we could do as a family when the children (from my first marriage) were younger. Together we've had to field years and years of people saying things like 'How are you feeling, Louise?' and then, without waiting for an answer, providing the answer 'Getting a little better every day,' or a variation on this. It's astonishing how powerfully people want to believe in a story about getting better, and how the real story, which is not a story about getting better, is not tolerated or allowed to be expressed by many people. I've also been beside Louise through years and years of unsolicited advice, often very well meant but often worse than useless. There's a common thread through a lot of this advice, which is given in the absence of the person listening to what Louise has to say. It also commonly positions her as an idiot or a mad person who for some reason will not have thought of some very obvious things. A good example is a recent exchange with a world-famous health professional (not in the field of orthopaedics, pain management or exercise) whom we've known for many years:

SHE: Louise, you know you must try swimming to help your hip – it's wonderful.

LOUISE: I used to swim every day before my hip replacement and I loved it, but for some reason I can't swim now. I've tried all sorts of things but swimming just does not work for me.

SHE: Swimming is the gentlest form of exercise and definitely better than any other form, and you should really try it.

LOUISE: Yes, you'd think so, but I've tried every stroke and variation and had help from the best exercise people we've been able to find, and it doesn't work for me, so I'm doing other kinds of exercise. I really miss swimming, and wish I could do it like other people who have pain can, but I can't.

SHE: When you swim, you must just keep your hips very, very steady and you'll find you won't have any pain ...

And so on and so on. I can understand and value the desire to help, but I resent the inability to listen. I become much more angry than Louise, who's more forgiving than I am. When colleagues and I were preparing a book on parenting a disabled child, I was able to use some of these experiences to write – helpfully, I hope – about how many people (and health professionals in particular) appear not to listen to parents of disabled children, not because of ill intent, but because of how hard it is for all of us to accept that bad things happen. We all expect doctors to make things better, and when they can't, they can become cut off from patients or stop listening. We all need to do more, not to blame doctors for this, but to help them behave differently.

Where is all this leading? There's another powerful story, especially in books written by disabled people and those who love them, that goes, 'I'm glad for the disability/the pain/the chronic illness. Without it I would not have learnt humility, patience, What Life Is Really All About,' and so on. Well, I'm not glad Louise lives with pain in the way she does. It has taught me things I wouldn't have known before, and I think the pain and the need to take it into account have made our close relationship even closer. But especially when the pain is bad for a long time, I resent it. I don't resent Louise, but I resent the pain. It sometimes feels that the pain is a third party in our relationship, an intruder we have to take account of – it's Louise, me and the pain. But would

I want to be married to someone else? Not at all. And I don't think my choice of Louise is a bad one for me – far from it. It's easy to see how my watching my father so closely when I was a child prepared me to be, I hope, an understanding and non-judgemental husband to a woman who lives with significant pain. But I also think I'm more than that. My life is not just a life of caregiving (despite my choice of career as a psychologist). I am not just Louise's caregiver; in fact she is my caregiver just as much as I am hers. Yes, the pain, the impairment, matters in our relationship, and it would be crazy not to admit this, but there's more to both of us, and to our life together, than what's wrong with her and what's wrong with me (thank goodness). Pain does not and never has defined Louise – she's fought her whole life not to be defined by pain. It doesn't define me either.

8

Careful With That Axe, Francine

One of my lesser-known talents is that I am able to take any dog, however well trained, and within a very short time turn the dog into an untrained animal. I have not had many dogs in my life but, to varying degrees, they have all been badly behaved. It is somewhat embarrassing to have badly behaved dogs, especially for a psychologist well versed in the principles of behaviour therapy, and at one time I considered turning this shameful weakness into a strength. I thought about opening a Dog Untraining School, at which over-regimented pets could become more able to express their true natures by learning to do uninhibited things like digging up plants and messing on carpets. I had to abandon my idea (for the time being, anyway) as it was just too far ahead of the market.

One of the uninhibited things dogs can do is bark incessantly, which is guaranteed to disturb the neighbours. When a woman named Francine lived next door to us in Cape Town, we had a dog who was just such a barker, and I was very careful to make sure that Bobo was not let out of the house between the hours of 8 p.m. and 8 a.m., because I didn't want the dog waking up the neighbours. He did bark more than he should during the day, though, and this enraged Francine. I thought she was fortunate that Bobo did not get into her treasured garden, with its perfectly tended lawns and its smelly but symmetrical rows of marigolds, and that he did not eat said marigolds or foul the lawns and concrete paths. Francine thought differently. 'I just can't take it,' she said. 'That dog of yours barks all day every day, and my nerves are just shattered.' The fact was that the dog did not bark all day every day, and I suspect Francine's nerves were shattered long before she met Bobo, but more about that later.

I did not like being on bad terms with my neighbours, and I was somewhat mollified by the fact that Francine was on very loud non-speaking terms with the man who lived across the road. The problem could not, I reasoned to myself, lie entirely with my untraining of Bobo. The Man Across The Road, whose name I never learnt, seemed to have his own difficulties in life. He objected passionately to non-organic gardening (very noble, I'm sure, but he was not wise to pick a fight with Francine and her geometric garden paradise on this issue), and he also parked his car in a way Francine did not like. 'There he goes again,' Francine would say, to nobody in particular and certainly not to The Man Across The Road. 'Parking like he owns the place, letting his weeds grow over his fence, taking no consideration – none at all! – of the rest of us.' And so on. I was more than a little afraid of Francine, partly because she reminded me so much of Granny and the Buchenwald Chicken in her use of her frailty as a weapon against all and sundry. But I'm pleased to say that all my practice losing at Scrabble to Auntie Lea in childhood stood me in good stead with Francine. I managed to ingratiate myself into her affections, and though we never became friends (that would have been a bridge too far), we managed to become neighbourly in the good sense of the word – keeping out of each other's way and waving pleasantly when we saw each other. I achieved this partly through interpersonal skill, but partly through something rather more devious and underhanded. For some reason, on one occasion when Francine was being particularly difficult, I remembered in my head the title of the unnerving Pink Floyd song 'Careful With That Axe, Eugene', complete with screaming by Roger Waters. I have never worked out whether the 'axe' referred to is slang for a guitar, but in any event the aggressive axe/guitar image is appropriate to the song. I used to listen to this song late at night on the radio in my room as a teenager, and at a time when my relationship with my grandmother was especially difficult. So it wasn't that surprising that I should link 'Careful With That Axe, Eugene' with my tussles with Francine. From that day on, in my mind and in that of my family, Francine's name became Careful With That Axe Francine, which we used to shorten to Careful. While we enjoyed using this nickname among ourselves, I'm grateful Francine never knew she had been given it.

I've had other neighbours and acquaintances who have suffered similar but less spectacular fates in naming as Francine did. A neighbour who would stop her car suddenly in the middle of the road if she saw any oncoming traffic (not pleasant if you were driving behind her), and who was clearly as terrified of driving as she was of greeting us, became Nervousina; I never did learn her real name. When Nervousina moved out, in moved Rex, who I thought was probably ex–Rhodesian military, and his wife, who always walked two steps behind him carrying all the parcels.

Though I felt very sympathetic to this woman, this did not stop me from renaming her: she became Long Sufferina. I'm not un-ambivalently proud of all these names, and I've noticed that there is something of a pattern to them. I tend to give names to older women whom I experience as difficult or especially vulnerable – and I'm the first to admit that there's a kind of cruelty in my doing this. Revenge of the grandson/great-nephew, I guess.

All the people to whom I have given names are, in my limited view of them anyway, difficult people or attached to difficult people or vulnerable in some way, and therefore I see them as fair game. There's an old joke among psychologists that there are only three kinds of psychologists in the world. The options are Painful Personality, Lack of Moral Fibre or Bad Blood. In the manner of the astrologers, I tend to put myself in the category of Painful Personality with Bad Blood rising, and this feels very apt to me. In fact, the silly categories feel remarkably apt to so many of my psychologist friends. Many of us have grown up with social difficulties (Painful Personality), without quite following the rules other people follow (Lack of Moral Fibre) or with mental illness in the family (Bad Blood). But while this joke about psychologists by psychologists is a bit of black humour, it raises other questions about how we understand people who may have disabilities that are not easily visible, disabilities that easily merge into things we call difficult or bad behaviour.

When we left Salisbury in 1966, Granny and Auntie Lea stayed on in their Rotten Row flat. Over the next few years, Granny became more and more depressed, missing her only son. (And life cooped up in a flat with the Buchenwald Chicken could not have been much fun anyway.) There was one psychiatrist in Salisbury at that time, a man I call Dr Hilarius (after the psychiatrist in Thomas Pynchon's *The Crying of Lot 49*), and he had to treat my grandmother. Many years later, Granny, a stranger to any stigma that may be associated with mental illness, would tell anyone who cared to listen, including bemused strangers on the bus, 'I had six shock treatments. I didn't know where I was.' This was always said very loudly (she was quite deaf by then) and while holding up all four fingers and thumb on one hand and her thumb on the other. Unless she had been misdiagnosed, Granny had suffered a major depressive episode after we left Salisbury, and was given electroconvulsive therapy for this. Aside from the six shock treatments, the prescribed treatment was for Granny to come and live with us in South Africa, thus opening a chapter of great misery for my family and for her, as we just did not get on, but Dr Hilarius said that this was what she needed. I've never forgiven Dr Hilarius for this, partly because it seemed to me that he never bothered to think of the implications of this move for both my grandmother and the rest of us, but mainly because I suspect that he wanted to be rid of a very difficult patient.

After Granny had been staying with us for some years in Johannesburg, my mother became increasingly unable to cope with the load and went to see her local general practitioner, a kind but unimaginative man. I was home from university and accompanied her to see the doctor, as she was worried he wouldn't believe her when she told him how impossible Granny was. She was right to worry. The kind but misguided doctor looked my mother in the eye, told her that things could not be so bad and that she must cope, and ended our memorable interview with the words 'Honour thy mother and thy father', which he intoned sonorously to my mother. He did, however, offer to see Granny to hear her side of the story (I think he was worried about elder abuse), and so we duly took Granny to his rooms the following week. He greeted us with a warm but patronising smile, and Granny went with him into his consulting room. Within ten minutes, the doctor emerged from his office and said all too loudly to his receptionist, 'Get this woman out of here!' He hadn't been able to bear even ten minutes with Granny in full sail, and I suspect Dr Hilarius had had a similar problem. Granny was, shall we say, not easy.

I have never stopped blaming Granny and the Chicken for being as difficult as they were. This is in sharp contrast to the way that I have never consciously blamed my father for his twisted feet. But is this fair? Granny, at least, had a diagnosed major mental illness, or what the disability movement would call a psychiatric disability. We know that one of the things that can happen when one grows up with a mental illness or psychiatric disability which is not diagnosed or treated is that one can develop ways to deal with one's difficulties, ways of coping, which are not always the easiest for others to manage. When I think of Granny, or of Careful With That Axe Francine with her obsessively neat and sterile garden, I'm struck by how hard we find it to make allowances for people's emotional difficulties – and I am one of those who should know better.

Even where serious mental illness is involved, we struggle with understanding other people and making allowances for their situation. People in the disability movement are keenly aware of the extra challenges faced by those who have what is known as 'hidden disability'. When we can see somebody limping or using a wheelchair, we know what we're dealing with; it's much more difficult to make allowances for things we can't see. A mother of a child with autism described to a co-researcher and me the consternation her son once caused in a shopping centre.[1] He was pacing a line in the tiles on the floor, and because of his disorder he would move anybody and anything out of the way of what he was doing. One person in the way was a woman in a miniskirt, whose interpretation of being touched on the thigh by this boy was understandably quite different from the correct one that she was simply something obstructing his path.

When we were working on the disability assessment tool at the HSRC, one of the things we had to take into account was the fact that people's ability to work may be profoundly affected by things we can't see. A person who has had a closed head injury affecting a particular part of the brain, for example, may speak perfectly rationally and intelligently, but may be unable to plan tasks for the day. The person may become enraged or tearful when frustrated. It's hard to see these problems for what they are, and I've no doubt that on occasion I have been irritated by the behaviour of someone with a neurological disorder. One of the most difficult-to-manage aspects of schizophrenia is not the hearing of voices or the delusions, but what are termed the 'negative symptoms' of schizophrenia. Many people with schizophrenia may have trouble getting out of bed in the morning or with motivating themselves to complete tasks. When we discussed symptoms like these with people who at the time were scheduled to sit on panels to determine whether people should be given disability grants, they struggled with this idea of negative symptoms. I don't think we ever got to a stage where they fully understood that negative symptoms can be part of an illness rather than a sign of moral failings or laziness.

And these moralistic ideas go along with our expectations about what people's appropriate social roles are. In the early days of a project on infant development in a very poor area, I spent a great deal of time training community health workers to recognise post-natal depression. The training went well, and by the end of the sessions all the health workers could reel off the symptoms of depression; they were all fired up to identify post-natal depression among the women they worked with and to refer them for appropriate treatment. The very next week, I did some supervision with one of the more gifted community health workers, one who had done well in the training. With great courage, she admitted to me that she was feeling very angry with one of her clients. 'She just sits there like a queen,' she said, 'while her poor husband runs around doing everything.' She told me the story of this woman, who had a baby and another child a few years older. The older child probably had some sort of developmental disability and was eating sand, and had also recently drunk the family's entire bottle of cooking oil. The infant was fretful and difficult to settle. Throughout this, the woman sat motionless on her bed with a sad expression on her face, while her husband rushed about, doing the best he could to look after the two children and his wife, and to cook food for the family. Hearing this story, I had little doubt that the mother was severely depressed, to the point of being immobile, and this was the conclusion we eventually came to and acted on, but this took some time. The community health worker explained to me that in her community men were generally absent and unsupportive, if not downright abusive. It was rare to see a man as helpful and caring as the husband of the depressed woman, and as we talked the community health worker confessed that she felt rather envious of this woman who had such a good husband. She also believed strongly that any woman who has such a good husband must behave appropriately to indicate to her husband that she appreciates all he is doing for her. Our discussion about the client and her depression was painful for the community health worker, as she realised the extent to which her feelings about this woman were determined not by what she had learnt the previous week about depression, but by her own experience of relationships between men and women in her community.

Because the boundaries between what may be termed bad behaviour and behaviour consequent on emotional difficulties are so porous, we struggle as a society to know when to make allowances for people's behaviour and when to hold them responsible for this behaviour. The rise of victim culture does not help. I was once contacted by a law firm putting together the defence for a man who was accused of murder. As I recall the story told to me by the lawyer, the man had met another man at a bar, and the two had then decided to go to the accused's home, where they had unprotected sex. In the morning, the accused man's sexual partner mentioned that he was HIV-positive. The accused went to his kitchen, found a knife and stabbed the sexual partner several times until he was dead. The lawyer asked whether I would be prepared to collect evidence to suggest to the court that the accused had acted in the heat of the moment, had been traumatised by the thought of possibly having contracted HIV, and should therefore not be convicted of a crime. I refused. I did not follow the case in any detail, and I don't know exactly what happened and what evidence was led in the court, but I heard later that another psychologist had submitted evidence to the court that the accused had been abused as a child and had been traumatised. Ultimately the man was acquitted. There may well have been more to the case than I know, and I am in no position to comment on the decision. But what I can say is that when we think about questions of morality and responsibility, the notion that emotional problems or bad experiences can exonerate one from responsibility is for me quite problematic. On the other hand, though, I am quite content to take brain disorders and mental illnesses into account when thinking about what people should be blamed for and what they should not be blamed for. But I don't always know when people have brain disorders, and given that we all have emotional difficulties, where do we draw the line?

My confusion over this issue is not a private matter – it affects how I treat other people. I once had a colleague who, to use a complicated professional expression, drove me round the bend. Sometimes she was good at her work and sometimes she was quite terrible at it, and it was unpredictable when she would do good work and when she would make enormous messes. The feedback on her teaching from students vacillated between absolutely glowing and downright appalling. Sometimes she was fully available to students and sometimes she did not even appear for class. She forgot many things, but not all things, and certainly nothing associated with her constant wish to climb the academic ladder. I knew she had some difficulties in her family, so I could understand her being distracted at times. I wondered whether she might have a drinking problem or some sort of neurological disorder. I also knew that my colleague disliked me – she disagreed with me theoretically on a number of issues, and she believed that I unfairly victimised her for minor issues and that I did not respect her academic prowess (which, when she was doing well, was considerable – she published many very good articles). I find it hard when people don't like me (not the worst of problems, but quite a serious one when one is in a position of authority over colleagues). I just did not know how to treat this colleague. Sometimes I would become enraged, sometimes I was sympathetic, and sometimes a dangerous cocktail of the two. I wrestled with my conscience about whether to raise with her the question of whether she was experiencing some intermittent memory problems, or perhaps had a drinking or drug problem (for which I had no evidence at all apart from the inconsistency in her behaviour). Not surprisingly, this colleague never knew where she stood with me, and she said so. We never managed to resolve anything between us. She subsequently moved away for a promotion and I was mollified (though I felt guilty) to hear that she caused similar distress to colleagues in her new place of employment. But the difficulties I had with her stay with me.

I don't think I'm alone in not knowing quite what to do about what may be psychiatric or neurological disability. The 'hidden disability' issue is a really tough one, especially when we can't see why somebody is being irritating or difficult, whether they are experiencing pain or just skiving off, whether they are having trouble hearing or are just not listening. It is even more difficult when the effects of impairment are sporadic and inconsistent, as they often are. We prefer people to be in their categories and to stay there, so we know what we're dealing with. But many people have fluctuating pain levels; they may be able to walk quite easily one day but not the next, and so on. It's easier to see any inconsistency as evidence of faking than as part of the difficulty of living with a fluctuating limitation on activity.

These issues are most clear in the case of impairments we can't see, but they do have bearing on how people live with impairments in general. I was at university with an arrogant and unpleasant young man, John, of whom we were all jealous, as he seemed to have two gifts of great use to him. John could attract any woman (or so it seemed) without any difficulty, and he was the master of excuses. He would always be late with work assignments but never got into trouble for this – in fact, he was a favourite with his lecturers. A year after John left university, he was involved in a serious motor accident which left him permanently disabled; he now has to walk with crutches. In his current job, John reports to a friend of mine who has known him only since the accident. John is a favourite with the female staff at work, but he is very poor on delivering his work on time. He refuses to do tedious jobs which all his fellow employees have to do, such as filling in time-billing forms. When confronted on his poor work performance, he accuses his superiors (including my friend) of discriminating against him on the basis of his disability. In this he gains tremendous support from some co-workers, who agree that he is badly treated. John's behaviour is divisive in the small consulting firm in which he works. Because my friend knows that I have an interest in disability rights, he often discusses with me his anguish over his failure to manage John properly. He worries that he is indeed disablist and lacking in understanding of disability, as John says. In these situations I am always grateful that I knew John before he was disabled. I can say with complete honesty that John's behaviour is entirely consistent with how he behaved as an undergraduate. I am sure his impairment causes him difficulties, but I can also cool-headedly see how he uses his impairment to his own ends. Had I not known John years ago, I would probably struggle much more to be clear about my feeling about what's going on with him.

The social model of disability requires us to think contextually and holistically about disability and the social situations in which it is experienced by all of us, and, as I've suggested, this is some-times easier said than done. But it's a mistake to think that the social model focuses only on barriers to social inclusion. The social model is also about the kinds of situations that make it easier for people to be included in society. In order to discuss this issue, I have no choice but to raise the profound question of what hair-dressers think.

One thing I thought I knew for certain growing up was that I would never be bald. My father had a full head of beautiful white hair, and I had a lot of curly and quite unruly hair, perfect for my youth in the 1970s. Sad to relate, I am now bald. Hair-dressing issues have become of little relevance to me, but when I did still have hair (and this was not that long ago), I used to have my hair cut by a very strange woman I'll call Crystal. About forty years old, Crystal was sweet and always friendly, but an unnerving feature of having my hair cut by her was that she never seemed to be looking at my head, which was worrying given that she would be wielding a variety of sharp instruments. She was excellent at cutting my bushy hair, but the minute I sat down she would begin to tell me dreamily how she had had visitations from aliens, she had been on extraterrestrial travels, and the world was about to end because of human greed. She heard messages from rocks and sometimes from trees, and the rock energy sometimes controlled her thoughts and actions. All of this was spoken about in a languid manner as she snipped at my hair, and though the hair never seemed to be her focus, my hair was always well cut. One day she showed me what to me looked like a ridiculous book with pictures of people with lines in different colours drawn around them – the lines, she told me, were the auras of the people, and the photographs had been taken by psychic cameras. Quite involuntarily, I chuckled at this, and Crystal became angry with me, but just for a moment, and then she continued with her dreamy monologue. Crystal had recently set up an internet connection at home (she was ahead of me on this one), and she told me how she now had contact with people of similar views and interests in all parts of the world, especially California. These relationships seemed more important to her than any she had locally – she lived alone, there seemed to be no partner in her life, and she did not go out anywhere, apart from to the supermarket and to work, as far as I could tell.

I have little doubt that if a psychiatrist (or I) were to have sat down with Crystal and put her through a standard diagnostic interview, she would have been diagnosed as psychotic. She heard things others did not hear, felt controlled by forces from the outside, and had beliefs out of keeping with those of her cultural group. There's always some difficulty in psychiatric diagnosis with whether beliefs held by someone which seem strange to the psychiatrist are actually part of the beliefs shared by another culture or subculture. In some groups, for example, it's considered quite crazy to believe that my contracting, say, tuberculosis, is because someone is jealous of me and is bewitching me; in other groups, this is a perfectly reasonable explanation and not at all strange. But there's a difference, a psychiatrist who once taught me used to say, between a subcultural belief and a belief shared by a group of crazy people who seek one another out! Regardless of the beliefs and hallucinations she may have had, Crystal was also quite withdrawn socially. Leaving aside the issue of whether she was technically psychotic or not, Crystal was a person out of step with many of the social roles one would expect from a woman of her age and social background. She reminded me of many people I'd seen in or at the fringes of psychiatric institutions. But as far as I knew, she had never received any treatment for mental disorder, and according to the social model it would be difficult to say she had a psychiatric disability – she was earning a good living and was well liked, as far as I could see, by clients and colleagues, though socially isolated otherwise. On the other hand, she had quickly made lots of internet friends. More important than anything else, she seemed quite happy and contented – happier than many people I find much less strange.

Part of why Crystal was so well able to cope despite what for another person might be serious symptoms was that she had her nice, dreamy manner and was pleasant and non-threatening to be with. It's often recommended that people who are a bit strange socially should be in jobs that do not involve too much social interaction, and in fact internet business has been a boon to many people with autism spectrum disorders, for example. But Crystal had chosen a job that involves working with people. When you think about it, though, Crystal's interactions with people, though quite intense, were structured around a specific task – she would begin her monologue as you sat down to have your hair styled and would stop as you left. The social rules of turn-taking in conversation were not really being followed, but because of the situation this was not as much of an issue as it might have been in other contexts. She had also chosen a profession in which there is tolerance for creativity and difference. Among her colleagues, for example, were two men who were both flamboyantly gay. One of the men called himself Alicia and was never seen without his eye make-up. Both these men were, as far as I could judge, single, and both looked older than Crystal. Another colleague was a woman who always dressed in black; she was heavily tattooed and had many piercings. Clients who came to this salon expected eccentricity, accepted it and probably (like me) found it part of the charm of the place.

For some time I would scratch my head wondering how Crystal could manage in the world, and if I am honest I must admit that I still worry that she might be vulnerable to exploitation and hurt by an unscrupulous person. But my overwhelming feeling about Crystal when I think about her now is one of admiration. She was just so clever to find the job she did and to make her niche where she did, to find a virtual social circle on the internet, and to have carved out a way of living happily and productively, if somewhat out of the mainstream. I imagine she was teased and shunned as a child and adolescent, and that there were times she (and her family) worried about how she would make her way in the world. There are so many worse things to do than to be a very good hairstylist, if one with a slightly odd way of dealing with the world. I doubt Crystal will ever be an entrepreneur or own her own hair salon, but there are millions of others who also won't. And she's just a shade away from so many people who can't find and keep work because of their psychiatric problems. Not all of these people are lucky enough to have a talent, and Crystal does have a talent, but I have met many talented people (including talented hairdressers, in fact) who have not been able to manage in the world.

Are there any lessons we can learn from the story of Crystal? I think there are. For behind the story of Crystal and her accomplishments, her ability to find a way in a world not built for her, there must be stories of people who were prepared to look beyond her oddness and to give her a chance to work and interact with people. All too often I hear people saying, 'We can't have disabled people here – it will upset the customers/children/adults/donor funders.' And though it is sometimes true that people will be upset, it's often our own worries, our own sense of upset, that we are responding to. People may be more accepting and more tolerant than we think, and that tolerance comes in part not from themselves but from the cues in the environment. If Crystal's colleagues had nervously apologised for her behaviour and assured me as a customer that I could have another stylist if I so wished, I might have become anxious and worried, and this would have put a barrier between me and Crystal. I was upset to read recently about complaints from some parents regarding a BBC children's television presenter who has one arm.[2] I have no doubt some children were indeed frightened when they saw the presenter, that some were worried that she was hurt. Parents of such children had a choice. Some chose to complain and to ask for the presenter to be removed from television; I'm sure there were others who reassured their children and told them about how people's bodies may differ from theirs. And there are also people with minds different from our own. Not all of them are as gentle or as personable as Crystal; not all of them are able to discuss their 'six shock treatments' with the same loud equanimity that my granny did. But there are things we can learn from them, things that can enrich our lives and make us grateful for what they can provide.

9

Activity and Development

I started my professional training as a clinical psychologist in 1980. I was twenty-four years old and inexperienced in the ways of the world, though growing up in my eccentric family had prepared me for dealing with a wide range of people. The director of the professional training programme was a very gifted psychologist who had done some innovative work in the field of intellectual disability, and wanted us to get some early exposure to the field. In the second week of our training, before we had seen any other clients, and before we had learnt any theory at professional level about psychological interventions, we had to spend the entire week working as nurse aides in a large institution for people with learning disabilities. Like the permanent nurse aides, we worked twelve-hour shifts, and spent five full days in the wards of the institution.

On our first day we arrived at the crumbling Victorian building very early in the morning (it was still dark), and without any preparation we were assigned to our wards. Having recently been selected for clinical training from large numbers of applicants, we were all keen to show how we were on top of things, able to handle anything professionally. One trainee in our group had previously worked as a psychiatric nurse in a large institution and had little difficulty slipping into the nurse-aide role; the rest of us had much more trouble. I can remember very little of that week, and what I do remember is not pleasant. I felt out of my depth and frightened, and there was no legitimate channel for discussing these feelings. One thing I do remember clearly is that one young man, who was very strong, grabbed my wrist and, without making any eye contact with me, manoeuvred my hand to open a desk drawer and to take out something he wanted. My wrist was hurt by the tightness of his grip and I did not know what to do. Watching this scene, the nurse aides on the ward had a laugh at my expense. They explained to me that this young man had severe autism as well as intellectual disability. His sense of other people was poor and he had been using my hand purely as a tool. He had not wanted to hurt me, but in his mind using my hand was similar to using a screwdriver to attach two pieces of wood with a screw.

Did I learn something from this experience? Definitely. But my unprepared colleagues and I, through being exposed in this brutal way to intellectual disability, by being forced into working with people we really had no way of understanding, learnt something else. All of us, apart from the colleague who had previously been a nurse, decided that we never wanted to work with people with intellectual disability – we were just too traumatised by the experience. I'm grateful that years later I came to have many other very positive experiences with people with intellectual disability, but it did take me years to get over the frightening and humiliating experience of that week at the institution.

If this were simply an account of a misguided attempt by a

psychologist to give students an experience of intellectual disability, it would not be an especially interesting story, but it is a story with echoes that I think remain important for how we think about disability and the people who choose to work with disabled people. The experience was, of course, located in a particular time – almost thirty years ago – and many things have changed since then. For one thing, we were trained at the tail end of a powerful encounter-group culture in some professions (including psychology), which fed on the idea that raw emotions, and strong aggression in particular, were what society covered up. If we were to be psychologists, the reasoning went, we must learn not to fear very strong feelings. And the way to help us face these fears was to expose us to emotionally difficult experiences, including the experience in the institution for people with intellectual disability, as well as very taxing encounter groups among ourselves in which high levels of emotion, including aggression, were encouraged. This is a very old-fashioned (not to say cruel) approach to the issue of emotional preparedness of mental health workers for their work. Its crudeness helps us understand something of what may be at the core of relationships between disabled people and some of the professionals and institutions tasked to assist them.

I'm glad that the experiences I had as a trainee in the institution would be unlikely to happen today. But the experiences do alert us to a central paradox in the way institutions and professionals may relate to disabled people, a paradox which is still very much with us. On the one hand, health professionals are the people we think of as having special knowledge about and empathy for disabled people. The entire profession of nursing, for example, is built on the idea that the main thing that nurses do is care for people. But a lot of what we expect nurses to do – especially when working with disabled people in institutions – is to make sure that people who behave in a socially unacceptable way, or who have bodies different from those of most people, are kept well out of sight of society in general. The role of nurses in these situations is as much about control as it is about care, and sometimes more so. In a similar way, we like to think that the role of the doctor is to cure people ('the doctor is going to make you better'), but doctors often deal with illnesses and life situations that they can't cure, and shouldn't be expected to be able to cure.

I know an elderly woman who has had serious and disabling neurological problems for much of her adult life. She finds it very difficult to accept that there is no cure for her condition, and so she goes from doctor to doctor, hoping each time for a cure and becoming more and more disappointed when this is not pro-vided. She was brought up to believe that if only she finds the right doctor her symptoms will disappear. So she has become the sort of patient doctors dread to see because she always wants the impossible, but it's not really her fault that she believes what she's been told about doctors and medicine. Part of what doctors try to do with her is to control her symptoms (which are very difficult to control), but also to control her behaviour so that she does not get too distressed and does not upset other people too much in her hopeless quest for what she was told doctors should be able to offer her.

So we have a situation in which there is some slippage in mean-ing among the words 'care', 'cure' and 'control', and professionals like me can get mixed up among different roles. I can see now that part of the lesson our trainer wanted to teach us when we were employed as nurse aides for a week was that there are these different roles. Part of being a health professional is not all about kindness and sweetness, but about doing difficult and dirty jobs that other people don't have to do, and about facing parts of life that others can get away with ignoring. We use lovely-sounding words for institutions – we even call them 'homes' – and sometimes they are very pleasant, good places. But no amount of hopeful use of names such as 'Sunny Acres', 'Happy Valley', 'Happiness House' or 'Serenity Place' can hide the anguish sometimes associated with families' decisions to place family members in institutions, or the sense that many people in institutions have of being cut off from the mainstream of life.

Granny had a terrible fear of being put into an old-age home, and would regularly accuse my parents of plotting and planning to put her into one. The irony was that in the last few years of her life she did decide to go into a home and was happier there than she had been for many years. Auntie Lea had developed Alzheimer's disease and was in the frail-care section of the home, where Granny could visit her every day. A further irony was that the very same Buchenwald Chicken who had tyrannised generations of relatives became, in her final years with dementia, sweet, malleable and contented. She was much loved by the nursing staff of the home. Like Granny, she too had feared moving into a home. There was a shadowy story behind this fear they both had, a fear I have never fully understood. I do know that, for some reason or other, their father had spent his last years and died in some sort of institution. It was described to me as an old-age home, but it may not have been. Granny and Auntie Lea lived in the Eastern Cape not far from a large psychiatric institution. Given that Poor Uncle Tubby committed suicide, that Granny had six shock treatments and that serious depression tends to run in families, I've often wondered whether my great-grandfather might have been put in that psychiatric institution and left there, as this was long before there were any effective treatments for severe depression. It's clear that the marriage between my great-grandparents broke down for some reason, whether it was mental disorder, conflict between them or something else. Could he, for example, have been a drinker, trying to deal with emotional difficulties with the only form of 'medicine' available to him? It's so long ago and not that important, but what Granny and Auntie Lea learnt was that institutions were places where people were put away and forgotten about.

Robben Island, where Nelson Mandela was incarcerated, was also once the site of an asylum for lunatics, lepers and the feeble-minded, to use the terms then current. We can learn something about the history of institutions when we consider how the asylum inmates were deliberately put on an island inaccessible to the general population. And we can see how the fear of contagion from people with leprosy could soon become fear of contagion of a more symbolic kind from people with psychiatric or intellectual disability.

Yet, when I read about the early days of psychiatry and the psychiatrists who worked in asylums,[1] I am struck by how the work of these early psychiatrists was such a humane project – an attempt to understand and to help. This humanity can also be seen in the writing of early psychiatrists such as Emil Kraepelin, who first described schizophrenia. Mixed in with progressive ideas about madness and disability were noble ideas about protecting people from a harsh society, and giving them an environment appropriate to their needs. Today we can easily comment on patronising approaches, on denying people their right to fulfil their potential in society. We tend to forget that 'asylum' is a word with positive connotations, in the sense of shelter or protection from the harshness and prejudice of the world.

To Granny, though, and to many others, institutions are where people are thrown away and forgotten. If disabled people are, as Tom Shakespeare says, 'dustbins for disavowal', institutions are seen as places where the rubbish is thrown, as far away from the public eye as possible. This perception persists in spite of the fact that so many institutions are very humane and well run, and we could not manage without them. But what do these ideas do to people who work in and stay in such places?

I was once part of a team providing some help to an institution for orphaned and abandoned infants and children. Some of the children had foetal alcohol syndrome, a condition caused by alcohol use in pregnancy and leading to distinctive physical features and intellectual disability. Others had no known impairments, but many of them were sad or aggressive, having experienced many difficulties in their short lives. The home was supposed to be a short-stay facility for infants under the age of two, but some children stayed there for three years and longer. As is so often the case with such institutions, facilities were poor and there were far too few staff members. Bath time at five in the evening was particularly difficult, as there would commonly be only one staff member on duty to bathe twenty toddlers and get them ready for bed. Anybody who has had even one child of this age will know that this time of day is often difficult for tired children and the adults who look after them; having to deal single-handedly with twenty tired children comes close to nightmare.

The staff of the institution were doing a heroic job under very difficult circumstances, and our group was, I think, able to help them. But what I learnt most from these hard-working women was about institutions and how they can operate. We were first called in to help at the institution because there had been some suggestion that staff members had been abusing children. We never found evidence for this, and we never got to the bottom of the story behind the allegations. It's unfortunately the case, though, that these days we think readily of abuse when we think about institutions caring for vulnerable people (just as we now tend to think of abuse when we think about Catholic priests, following all the scandals in the USA in particular). The staff, as do all staff in such institutions, knew about the lurking suspicion of abuse, and though it is quite possible that there might have been abusers among the staff, what was striking was how this spoilt identity – that of carer-turned-abuser – dogged the lives of all these women. They could not get away from the fact that people might think the worst of them. Living with this sort of constant suspicion over one's head (whether it is justified or not, whether it is expressed or not) can be corrosive and alienating. Paradoxically, it can also make the way in which carers do their jobs much worse and – yes – more abusive. The relationship between carer and charge is set up as potentially hostile and exploitative, and carers can defend themselves against this by not treating the children as individuals, by focusing on important routine tasks at the expense of emotional involvement (making sure that children are clean, for example, but not making contact with them as people) and by following institutional rules slavishly and meticulously. There's nothing at all wrong with following rules, and a busy and overburdened institution needs rules to be followed in order to function, but when rules are everything, the important human side of things can get lost.

One of the first things my colleagues and I noticed when we came to work at the institution was that the staff members addressed one another as 'mummy', as in 'Mummy, you were late for work today,' or 'Mummy, your child is calling for you.' There was something endearing about this, with all these women calling one another the name for the person they wished the children had but had lost, and wishing that it were true that every child had his or her own 'mummy' ('your' child). But we quickly became confused. In a place where every adult is 'mummy', it's difficult to know who's speaking to whom, or about whom. We also learnt that the staff were very concerned about being fair and not showing favouritism to any child, which was admirable. But there were consequences to this. No child had any toys of his or her own; the children did not have their own clothes. Nothing at all was individually owned, or associated with any particular child. This made the institution much easier to run. When, for example, the time came to dress the children, there was a large pile of clean clothing and all the staff had to do was to take from the pile any clothing that fitted the children. There were no worries about lost socks or shirts, no tantrums about favourite teddy bears or comfort blankets going missing. The system worked. But the sadness – the tragedy – of the situation was the neglect of the children's important need for attachment, for individuality, to be special in their own right, all of which are crucial for development, including, it appears from the latest science, brain development. Here were heroic women working extremely hard under difficult circumstances, doing work all day and every day that I certainly would struggle to do, caring deeply for the children (I have no doubt of this, having got to know many of them over a long period), being kind and fair, but not giving the children what they needed.

It's all too easy just to get angry about this situation, a situation which is repeated again and again across different institutions to varying degrees. There are also many stories of people who rush into such situations and try to take over, to make things better in a flurry of new activity. And many of these stories have sad endings, with the enthusiastic 'new broom' becoming demoralised and cynical, and the situation reverting to how it was before, with long-serving staff saying, 'We told you so. This is the only way this place can work.' The issues here are partly issues of resources – with much more money and many more staff members, much more can be done. (I love the old joke, especially pertinent in South Africa, that suggests we need a new way of generating money: Let's give proper money to care work, to education and to disability services, and when we need to buy a new warship or aircraft carrier, we can have a cake sale to raise funds for it.) Lack of resources is at the heart of the problems of places like the institution I'm discussing, but the neglect and the deprivation have emotional consequences too, for both staff and children.

What was at stake for these caregivers in their apparent inability or reluctance to form individual attachments with the children? Why were these attachments so hard for them? I can't pretend to have a full answer for this, but I think there were a number of things happening. First, the staff were worried about being overburdened by the needs of the children. If one allows oneself to engage with what just one of these children needs, it can feel as if there is a bottomless pit of need – and, indeed, there is nothing anyone can do to put right the wrongs that have happened to an abandoned child. Second, the staff were concerned about fairness and doing what was right by all the children. There could have been a fear that if a staff member became attached to a particular child, the caregiver would not be available to others, which would be inequitable. Then there could have been the fear of loss. It is hard to become attached to someone, even to a child, when you know that person will soon be gone and out of your life. Work with abandoned children evokes all our own experiences of loneliness and abandonment, experiences we have all had to varying degrees, as loss is part of life. So these caregivers, who were kind and concerned people, put efficiency and control before caring, as caring of the individual kind was too difficult in so many ways. As I've mentioned, in our time working with this institution we never got to the bottom of the allegations about the abuse of the children. We did learn, though, about the deep fear that many good caregivers had that their efficient work – the best they could do physically and emotionally – was not equal to the individual needs of the children; that this in itself constituted a kind of abuse. When we think about this microcosm of institutional care in a context of scarce resources, it is small wonder that many people who have lived in institutions, including disabled people, are so angry about what institutions cannot give. There's no doubt in my mind that there are abusive people and abusive institutions, and we need to be vigilant about these and stop abuse.

But there are also so many good people trying their best who become part of things that are not good for those who should be cared for and who deserve better.

It is human to feel uncomfortable about pain and about those situations in which life does not meet our expectations. And it is human for organisations and institutions that deal with difficulties in life to defend themselves and their staff against difficult feelings, and against the disappointment that many people feel when they can't do more. Isabel Menzies Lyth helped pioneer thinking on how institutions and professionals defend against difficult feelings, focusing much of her work on the routinisation and bureaucratisation of nursing in the UK.[2] She showed how caregiving professionals develop rules and procedures to the point where policies and procedures take precedence over feelings and over care. Anyone who has been treated in an efficient but cold and impersonal health-care centre will have a sense of what she was talking about. In work that follows the tradition established by Menzies Lyth, people began to see how institutions often take on the characteristics of the issues they are built to deal with. When I was part of a group working with a school catering for deaf children, for example, we found that staff complained repeatedly that colleagues did not listen to them, and never really heard what they said. Our key work here was on communication, as poor communication among staff negatively affected what was happening with the children.

Another organisation I worked with did not deal with disability or illness as they are commonly understood. This organisation worked with students who were disadvantaged by the inadequate skills they had learnt in the apartheid-era school system. Its educational programme was designed to develop the educational abilities of these students very rapidly, so they would be more successful in the labour market. The staff of this organisation was made up of talented and highly qualified educators, and they had a good vision of what they wanted to do. However, my colleagues and I found in working with them that just as they were offering accelerated learning to their students, the staff members were working more and more quickly and busily. Everything in the institution was rushed and rapid, with the result that staff (and students) became very tired but could not really speak about their tiredness and need for rest. Part of what we tried to do was to help the organisation to slow down and look after itself so that the difficult work could continue. One of the challenges associated with this sort of intervention is that when people are very committed to doing good things, and are also exhausted and out of touch with their own creativity, being overtired and stressed becomes the only way that people get a sense that they are doing any good at all. The aim of the work, which in this case was to help students to learn, can subtly be replaced with a new unspoken aim, which is to work so hard as to become exhausted. Nobody consciously wants this to be the aim of what they do, but this is what can and does happen.

The most poignant experience I've had, related to how organisations try to protect themselves and disabled people they work with from difficult feelings and realities, came from some consultation I and some colleagues did with an organisation that assists people with intellectual disability. This organisation had a well-deserved reputation of being an innovator in contributing to realising the rights of people with intellectual disability, and it offered a number of highly respected programmes. One of the organisation's concerns, and rightly so, was that of how to help find work with dignity for people with intellectual disability, and it was among the first to argue that people with intellectual disability must where possible work in integrated workplaces and on the open labour market. But the organisation also believed, as was the dominant view at the time, that some people had a range of difficulties which meant that they were best placed for work in sheltered and protected workshops. The organisation had been very successful in winning contracts for repetitive but important work with major manufacturers and retailers, and ran a number of small industries that were sought after by businesses. When we started working with this organisation, it was one of the few of its kind managing to survive in the harsh new environment where everything is a business – in the post-Thatcher world, even public hospitals or workshops that cater to the needs of people deemed unable to function on the open labour market need to justify their existence on the basis of turning a profit. Much as this organisation, like me, found this new profit-driven imperative in the care 'industry' distasteful, it was able to meet the demands of the market. In addition, the people who worked in the workshops seemed relaxed, happy, well cared for and proud of what they had been able to achieve.

There was one group, though, that seemed out of place. With a fixed smile, the social worker at the organisation took us to a corner of the workshop. 'This,' she said, 'is our activity and development section!' She explained that this was a special section of the workshop where people who had particular needs were given extra activities and added opportunities to develop. From the words she used and the delighted smile on her face, one might have expected that the social worker was telling us about the part of the workshop where the people with the very best work potential were accommodated and given special attention to maximise their strengths in line with their extra abilities. The part of the workshop the social worker was showing us, though, was dark and dingy, and there was not much going on. A few people were sitting there pushing around bits of debris and refuse from other sections of the workshop. There was no babble of chatting while work was happening, and the people who were sitting around clearly had difficulty communicating. They were quiet, clean and well cared for, but they did not seem to be doing anything purposeful. In terms of the way occupational therapists think about the importance of everyday activity as life- and identity-enhancing, these people did not seem to be engaged in much activity, nor were they developing in any way. Clearly, these were the people at the workshop who had the most severe impairments and whose care needs were the greatest. They would never be active contributors to this profit-making workshop – they could not contribute as many others could. Far from being the 'activity and development' section, the section where they were cared for was, if anything, the 'inactivity and lack of development' section. Even as I write these words I feel embarrassed and guilty – how dare I say these things, especially in the context of talk about disability (talk I believe in) which emphasises achievement of rights, ability and empowerment? What will people think of me as I talk about 'inactivity and lack of development'? Well, these feelings of mine, which make me want to erase this bit of writing and to change my chapter (after all, nobody will know if I just don't talk about this), are an important key to some of the issues faced by the organisation and by the social worker who, as she saw our shock at what we saw in the activity and development section, kept on smiling, her smile now looking like a grimace.

The social worker was good at her work, and she was no fool. She knew that in a sense we had reached a moment she must have been dreading, but a moment she must have known was coming – an 'Emperor's New Clothes' moment, in which any-one not schooled in well-meaning doublespeak would know that the activity and development section was nothing of the kind. Her fixed smile now read to me like an appeal not to point out the obvious, an appeal to collude in what we all knew was not the truth, for the sake of protecting … what? This good woman, I think, felt ashamed that she was not able to do more for the people in this section. The language of Margaret Thatcher's mar-ket and the talk of empowerment for disabled people – strange bedfellows indeed – had conspired to make shameful the fact that empowerment, productivity and renewed ability were not possible for everyone. So many people with disabilities can, if properly supported, do better than they have been doing, and most people benefit from being challenged and supported to do more. But not everybody can do work that is economically profitable when all necessary support costs are factored in, especially where resources are scarce. This is a fact (though one that I am sure will be disputed by many). And it's unhelpful and dangerous not to allow this possibility, and to make people feel guilty when they stare the possibility in the face. We like to lay blame when things do not get better, when people who are supposed to help can't help, but this is not useful or productive.

It's admirable and desirable that institutions try to make people's lives better. One of the paradoxes of the 'Sunny Acres' story, however, is that we tend to use such resolutely euphemistic language, to keep our smiles fixed, only when we are all afraid that the reality may be somewhat different (I have not yet seen a 'Happiness House' venture capital firm). And this worry that we have about life not always being what we want has implications for all of us: we may expect too much from professionals and institutions, and in response professionals and institutions may become less caring than they could be. There is now such great emphasis on participation and community living for disabled people that we tend to have a knee-jerk negative view of institutions, and this can hurt people too. Are there unkind, abusive people who choose to work in institutions? Yes, there are, just as there are unkind, abusive people in other walks of life. But we need to do more to understand the dynamics of institutions, and the kinds of unrealistic expectations we have of professionals, if we are going to achieve the best we can for disabled people, and others.

IO

Valid and Reliable

There's a belief among research psychologists that if there is something worrying you as a psychologist or even as a person, the best way to address this worry is through 'research-mindedness' – that is, dealing with the issue through psychological research. It's hardly surprising given my history that I would become interested in disability-related research.

When I started working in the disability field, a number of colleagues advised me not to do so. They told me that disability research is so politicised, and there is so much aggression against able-bodied researchers from disabled people, that it's not worth doing this kind of work. Furthermore, disability research did not have a reputation for being very strong methodologically and was not very high-status for psychologists. On the basis of this, well-meaning colleagues said, I should really not be jeopardising my career by entering a new and difficult field – why didn't I just build on my existing strengths? After all, I had enough research and writing under my belt that I did not need to do disability-related research in order to establish a research career. I've thought of this advice many times over the past few years, especially at times when I've felt demoralised and even hurt by some of the processes I have experienced in disability research. But I'm not one to be put off getting involved in a field because it's difficult to work in or because it's low-status. In the 1980s I had been advised not to get involved in the field of community psychology, because it was academically weak relative to some other fields in psychology. With characteristic stubbornness I stuck with community psychology, and I commented in my inaugural lecture at UCT in 1996 that if you stick around on the margins for long enough the centre will move to you. This is certainly what happened with community psychology for a brief period around the transition to democracy in 1994, but it's moving out of fashion again quite fast. But the truth of the matter of my involvement in disability research was that I had almost no conscious choice – working in the disability field was something I just had to do. When frustrated with the field, I threaten to my long-suffering family that I am not going to do any more disability-related research, but they have learnt not to believe me – this is where I am, and part of who I am, for now. But my frustrations with disability research (and they are substantial) do not come from where I was warned they would come.

Not long ago I was principal investigator on a huge disability-related project that was much too big for any one organisation to tackle. Because of the scope of the project, I had to subcontract work to various individuals and organisations, and on the whole the experience was a positive one – I made a number of close friends through that research process. The highest fees charged, though, were by a well-known research organisation which enjoyed considerable credibility with the disability sector in South Africa.

Not only did this organisation charge more than others, its representative, whom I'll call Mark, also made very clear in meetings that his organisation's work was better than anyone else's, and I had to manage some of the fallout from situations when Mark insulted other partners. It was certainly true that Mark's organisation had a raft of research reports which were greatly valued by the disability sector, and it was for this reason that I was happy to pay Mark and his organisation more for their services than I did for those of other partners, including one partner who was well known internationally in the disability-research world, and who had done path-breaking work for a major international agency, work which is being used throughout the world.

Meetings with Mark were difficult, as we braced ourselves for his lectures about how we did not understand the importance of participatory processes with the disability sector, how important it was to understand empowerment, and so on ad nauseam. It was also very difficult to discuss with him issues of substance to the research, apart from his repeatedly reminding us of the wonderful work his organisation had already done for the sector. As with many other research processes I have been involved in, on this project our relationship with the disability sector itself was good, and really not difficult to manage; however, our relationship with Mark, a self-appointed able-bodied spokesperson for disabled people and their champion against disablist and right-wing researchers like myself, was extremely difficult. To make matters worse, I began to feel more and more uncomfortable, as it seemed to me that Mark was unable to engage with anything other than the politics of disability research, and that with sweet rudeness he was turning any conversation we might have had away from the substance of what we were paying him a lot of money to do. For probably far too long, I kept my counsel, and admonished myself for my bad thoughts. Mark and his organisation were well known and they would surely deliver good work, work we could use.

When Mark finally gave me the report on the work he had been doing for us, my worst fears were realised. There were two major problems with what he handed over. First, quite a lot of what was in the report seemed to be cut and pasted from material his organisation had previously produced and was already in the public domain. I had expected him to build on this work, but I did not think it fair that my project should have to pay again for work that had already been paid for as part of previous research projects. More seriously, though, it was clear that Mark had no basic understanding of some key technical terms he was using in his report. This was not a matter of interpretation – these were terms all basic texts on research methods agree on. One of Mark's more memorable statements in what he produced for us was that it was possible to develop methods of assessment of complex variables in the disability field which were completely valid, completely reliable, and could be administered and scored by people with only a few days' training.

Anybody who knows anything about assessment theory knows that no form of measurement of complex attributes can be completely accurate (or, to use the technical term, valid). It is also never possible to get 100 per cent agreement across raters for complex assessment instruments – what technically is called inter-rater reliability is never complete. Reliability is further threatened when the people doing the assessments are inexperienced and have limited education. These conclusions have been reached by the best minds in the assessment field worldwide, and are not news to anyone with the most basic understanding of the principles of assessment. Let me give an example. Say, for example, we want to be able to predict how many years and months a child with serious learning difficulties would be likely to stay in mainstream schooling. If we had a completely valid and reliable measure to predict this, we would be able to say with 100 per cent certainty that the child would spend exactly x years and y months in mainstream schooling. This view would be agreed on by all experts and, if Mark's promise were to be realised, exactly the same conclusion would be reached by people with only a few days' training and with no previous experience in doing assessments of this kind.

This kind of reliability, validity and ease of measurement is something we all hope for, and I think that some people honestly believe that it's possible to achieve it. (It amazes me how often people think that because I am a psychologist I can actually read their minds.) We all have a great need and wish for certainty, for there to be experts who can help us out of all our uncertainty. But it's the difficult role of experts not to collude with this wish, but to help people understand what experts can and can't do. The claims Mark was making, paradoxically, were exactly the claims to some mysterious 'scientific' knowledge, claims which people who are concerned about the democratisation of knowledge should not be making. Not only was he promising the impossible (and basing a lot of his arguments on a promise that could never be fulfilled), he was, as far as I could see, making claims for expertise which no expert actually has. The constituency for which Mark was accustomed to preparing reports, the disability sector in South

Africa, was dominated by people with a range of excellent skills but with little advanced (if any) training in research methods. It was doubly important, therefore, to be very clear with this sector about what was and was not achievable. We all wish for good things from experts in fields in which we are not expert; it is up to the experts to tell the rest of us what they can and can't do. In the heady sense of possibility in the young South African democracy, furthermore, people wanted to hear that the impossible was possible – and in the Mandela era, in some ways it felt that it was. Mark's claims were not all that different from a slew of other claims for 'delivery' which have since not been met in South Africa, but anyone not understanding that he was promising the impossible would have been impressed by what he said he could do. They would also have thought, quite reasonably, that others who said they could not offer completely valid and reliable measurements conducted by inexperienced and relatively untrained raters must have been worse at research than Mark was, as they could offer less.

I asked Mark to change his report for us, based as it was on an incorrect understanding of fundamental research principles. He refused and asked for clarification. I sent him a number of references which showed that he was using concepts incorrectly. Again he refused and asked for clarification. It was clear to me that either he had not read my comments and background information or he had not understood them. He was clearly angry, and pointed out for the umpteenth time that his organisation was a leader in the disability-research field. I will never forget a particularly unpleasant telephone conference during which Mark refused to acknowledge that there was any problem with his work and during which I was told by his superior that I obviously did not understand what the process of progressive research consultation was. My crime was that I was (allegedly) politically conservative or reactionary, and this was why I was not satisfied with work that was based on wrong ideas (this was not a matter of opinion – Mark did not or would not understand the principles he was using). Had I 'understood' progressive research consultation, I would have accepted Mark's work without demur. What a sad state of affairs. We paid Mark and his organisation a generous proportion of what we had promised to pay them on delivery of usable material, and employed a competent researcher (who did a good job) to redo the work. This was a costly and painful lesson in some of the politics of disability research, and there was not a single disabled person involved in the conflict.

It's possible to make too much of this single incident. In retrospect, I feel quite sorry for Mark, who was so clearly out of his depth in the kind of work we were asking him to do. His loud protests about the wonderful work he and his colleagues had done (and they had indeed done some fine work) can be read with the wisdom of hindsight as a frantic attempt to cover up his inadequacies, and his condescension to people much more experienced than he was should have been read by us as, if anything, a plea for help. I should have recognised these signs earlier and I should have done more to avert the crisis that developed. But though this is just one case involving one person, there are echoes of this experience in many places, and I'll come to some of these echoes later. The key question for me here is how disability politics came to enable the difficulties between Mark on the one hand and my colleagues and me on the other. We were all hurt by this experience, and it's easy to see the experience as no more than something personal, but I think there's a much bigger political message to learn from this.

The disability movement, with its emphasis on the social model and on the political and social oppression at the heart of many of the difficulties experienced by disabled people, has done us all a great service. But when participatory processes come to replace the content of what researchers can and should be doing in service of the movement, things can go seriously wrong. If working in service of the disability movement is only about empowering processes and nothing more, we lose precisely what researchers can and should have to offer: expertise and an approach to knowledge that is not available within the disability movement already. As more and more disabled researchers enter the field, the issue of able-bodied researchers having to be brought in to help will probably dissipate to some degree; but in the parts of the world where I work, able-bodied researchers are still very much needed. British disability activist Tom Shakespeare contends that even in Britain the dominant emphasis of a particular political approach to disability has been detrimental to good disability research. He argues that there has been an impasse in disability research, and says:

> While I value the achievements which have been won through the close alliance of disability politics and disability research, I believe that the weaknesses of the British approach now outweigh the benefits. Translation of ideas and ideologies from activism to academia has not been accompanied by a sufficient process of self-criticism, testing and empirical verification.

The social model of disability which has successfully inspired
generations of activists has largely failed to produce good
empirical research.[1]

Shakespeare talks about an insufficient process of 'self-criticism,
testing and empirical justification' in British disability research,
and there are many examples I can cite which suggest that his
words are relevant to disability research in the South African
context. What's going on here? One thing I have learnt as a
psychologist and researcher living in South Africa during the
transition to democracy is that it is much easier to be part of an
opposition critical of what the mainstream is doing than it is to
have the power and ability to do things oneself. So in the 1980s
and early 1990s, I could write very confidently about all the shortcomings of the mental health system under apartheid; nowadays,
I have to admit that though I was right about the injustices of
apartheid mental health services and systems, I really don't know
the best way to run health services in our democracy. I'm great
on principles, but not as good on detail and on dealing with the
multiple constraints that exist. We progressive researchers forged
our identities in opposition; it's difficult now that we find we can't
deliver everything we wish we could. One way of hiding these
difficulties is to keep playing identity politics – to hide our lack
of substance in a somewhat threadbare but still just attainable
revolutionary style. These issues are much more complex and
difficult across divides of race, class, gender and disability. It's
hard for people with privilege, people like Mark and me (both of
us are white and privileged), to say to people who have not had
our advantages that we can't do everything we'd like to do for

disabled people, that good researchers must on occasion provide information people don't want or don't like, and must on occasion say that we can't provide the information people wish we could provide.

As background to talking more about how this issue plays out in disability politics in particular, I think it's helpful to talk about some experiences I've had which do not relate directly to disability issues but which do speak to the politics of participation and knowledge in South Africa. I once attended a participatory meeting to help inform a parastatal about the best way to help women and girls who had been sexually abused. The wish was to hear 'from the community', and to understand the problem 'from the bottom up'. The participants broke up into groups to discuss our experiences and recommendations. One of the women in my group was there representing a gender justice organisation, but the week before she had had a dreadful experience – her granddaughter had been raped and she had been very badly treated at the hospital to which she had been taken. This woman was clearly extremely upset, and justifiably so. We spent our group time listening to her story and allowing her to tell us of the horrors she had experienced. When the time came for the different groups to give feedback from their deliberations, the very articulate spokesperson from our group spoke with empathy and passion about what had happened to our group member and her granddaughter. He recommended that priority be given to investigating the hospital at which they had had such a terrible, re-traumatising experience. Such was the power of what our group spokesperson said that when it came to listing in order the priorities coming out of the meeting as a whole, the issue of investigating this hospital made it to the top of the list. Now it would certainly be admirable to investigate what happened at this hospital. It would also be accurate to say that the recommendation that this investigation be given top priority was the result of a well-run participatory process. But as a researcher, as a citizen interested in the big picture of what we should be doing about sexual violence in the country, I am not at all sure that investigating one hospital should be at the top of the list. We need, I think, a discussion that goes beyond a performance of small-group participation and which considers different ways of thinking about how to glean information from the 'community'.

A second example which strikes me involved my participation in a disciplinary hearing for a health professional accused of financial impropriety. I and a number of other professional colleagues were asked to attend a hearing at which this professional was accused of defrauding clients and medical aid schemes. The allegations were serious, and there were heated debates and discussions about what should be done. We eventually reached a consensus about what to recommend. As we were about to leave, I turned to the one person who had not said a word all day. He had spent most of the day looking out of the window, seemingly disengaged from the process, and I assumed that he was some sort of official who was there in an administrative capacity. 'What is your role here?' I asked. 'Well,' he said, 'I am the community representative.' It turned out that this man, who had a legal qualification, spent some of his professional time going from disciplinary hearing to disciplinary hearing. He was compensated for his time and was there, as he said, to represent the community. When I asked him how he fed back his experiences to the community, he looked bemused and told me again that he was the community representative. I don't know if he was more active in other hearings than in the one we had been in that day, in which he had not said a word. It seemed to me, though, that there was something wrong here. In our democracy we value participation by citizens, and it's important that ordinary people have access to the world of powerful people like professionals. I could see exactly why there was a provision for a community representative on the committee, but only in the moment of this discussion with just such a person did I realise that for there to be true community participation, there has to be more than just a person called a 'community representative' present. There also has to be a complex (and expensive) process whereby the links between the representative and the 'community' (whatever that is) are made explicit.

This second example is much less cynical than a third example of which I have heard. I understand that for one of the professions in South Africa, there were elections for most of the positions on the professional board. The previous chair of the board had been so unpopular that she was not elected to the board. The government minister responsible for this board immediately appointed the person who was so clearly out of favour with the profession as a 'community representative' on the professional board. This action made a mockery of the idea of a community representative, as the person appointed by the minister was a member of the profession and very unpopular within it.

But even if we leave aside this last example of manipulation of the concept of participation for political ends, it is still clear that the concept is an extremely complex one. And in any sector, including the disability sector, it's important not to valorise participatory processes without examining them closely and without looking carefully at what these processes can and can't achieve. One thing that participation cannot achieve on its own is technical excellence in research. I have no reason to doubt, for example, that Mark's work and that of his colleagues was greatly valued by leading figures in the disability movement, but this does not mean that Mark understood what he was doing in terms of the esoteric knowledge that people gain as they learn about research.

And there's something difficult and painful here, at the nub, I think, of relationships between able-bodied researchers and the bulk of disabled people. The fact is that I, as an able-bodied white man who grew up in privilege, have had many advantages most disabled people have not had. This has given me access to an excellent education and to knowledge not all disabled people have had access to. The same goes for most of my able-bodied researcher colleagues. What should we do with this privilege? In Chapter 3 I spoke about how claims about being inside or outside the world of disabled people can lead to problems in how disabled and non-disabled people relate to one another. When it comes to issues of research and the important questions disabled people need answers to, things become more serious. Just as in the 1980s I was part of an audience who loudly applauded a trade unionist for insulting a group of well-meaning mental health professionals, I think there is a danger that competent researchers, in the interests of 'respecting' disabled people, may withdraw what they have to offer that is of use to the disability movement.

Does this really happen? And if it does happen, how does it happen? I believe it does happen, and I believe the reasons it happens are partly political and partly emotional. I am on shaky ground, I'm well aware, attributing emotional motives to other people, especially when I have not checked with them whether my wild analysis is correct or not, but I can, I hope, use my own convoluted feelings about disability and my place in relation to the disability movement to make some suggestions about what may be going on, and not just for me.

It's painful to think that I have many privileges and skills that others don't have. I have spent a lot of my life trying to take responsibility for my privilege and to give back to others in return for what I have. But the fact is that I give back only what suits me – I choose, for example, to live a middle-class life and not to share my income with others. It's also true that, whatever I do, I can't give back what privilege has given me. When I am confronted with my own privilege and power, my impulse is to minimise this, even to pretend that I don't have what I do have. I know I fool nobody with this, least of all myself, and it has certainly got me into trouble. For example, I had a very bruising experience many years ago with a black colleague from a historic-ally black university. I was supervising this colleague's research, and I struggled to be critical of what she was doing as I was so aware of the fact that my journey to academia had been so much easier than hers had been. The upshot of this was that this col-league felt abandoned by me, that I was not really interested in her, that I did not take her seriously. She was wrong, but I can see where she got the idea that I didn't care. The reality was that I cared far too much. In my work with the disability movement, I have indulged in the same game of trying to make things better between me and the movement by playing down my abilities and almost pretending to know less than I do know. There's a real dilemma for me about how to balance what I have to offer with not being dominating, about how to listen without silencing myself, about respecting other views without disrespecting my own. I feel this dilemma in my body, viscerally, and for me it's not that different from the dilemmas I felt as a boy growing up with my disabled father, with the way in which I punished both him and myself with the weakness of my own body. I make no apology for being involved in disability research as a way of trying to fix some difficulties, some pain, I had growing up. But what I need to do is to work as hard as I can not just to reproduce my past in another arena, but to use my experience of having a second chance, not to repair what happened to me in my childhood, to make it up to my long-dead father, but to put something right, to do something right, to use the power I have in my mind and my body to make things better.

I don't know if I can do this, or if it's a case of hubris to even dream that I can, but I am so fundamentally aware of the pull in the opposite direction, the pull towards covering all difficulties over, the pull to collusion, the pull to wasting what I can offer in a pretence of offering something. How can and does this happen? It's quite simple really. I engage in an implicit contract with disabled people that goes like this: 'I'll pretend not to notice that your disability and impairment, your experience of inferior education, your exclusion from quality education, matter, if you'll agree not to notice that I have privileges you don't have. Let's do it this way: I'll offer you nothing useful, and this won't make either of us feel uncomfortable about our relative power status, and we'll pretend that this nothing I have given you is quite enough.' There's something quite macabre about this deal – why on earth would I, or anyone else, not want to offer what we have to offer? But I know it's a deal that is very attractive to me, and it's a deal which, if I succumbed to it, would make me more popular and less controversial among some disabled people and some non-disabled researchers. Because if we can foster an illusion that we are all just the same, that we as researchers know no more than the disability movement knows already, that we will always agree with whoever talks the loudest in meetings with the movement, then we won't have to face the pain and the responsibility of difference. This process of collusion would look like an ideal mode of participation – everyone comfortably together, everyone sharing things acceptable to everyone else, but with nobody having to endure the pain of difference and the anxiety and discomfort which for me must be the basis for any real learning.

I can't say for sure whether any of these issues occupy the minds of other able-bodied researchers like me, but I think they may. I have had some conflict with some other researchers over the nature and process of disability research which suggests to me that these issues may be alive for them too. At a meeting on the future of disability research a few years ago, I commented that one of the difficulties with the emphasis on participatory approaches in disability research was that some researchers with excellent skills would not have the time or the interest to do disability-related research. If the rights of disabled people are to be realised, we need the research skills of, for example, engineers who specialise in transport and road construction, architects who design low-cost housing and public buildings, economists who understand small-business development. One of my colleagues, a person of whom I am very fond, and who has done more than most to facilitate good participatory research with the disability movement, seemed discomfited by what I said. She pointed out in some detail that there are knowledges which have been subjugated and driven from the mainstream; our work as researchers, she said, is to join hands with disabled people to help them uncover knowledge they have always had but were not aware of.

I have no problem with this view as far as it goes – I've had many experiences with community groups and with disabled people's organisations when I've been part of an exciting process whereby people have discovered that they have knowledge and expertise that they didn't realise they had. These moments are wonderfully transformative, and are to be treasured. Anybody who has any doubts about the nature of the oppression of disabled people should have the privilege of being present at moments when disabled people who think they have nothing to offer, who think they know nothing, realise that they know much more than they have given themselves credit for. These moments can feel miraculous. But there must be more to research than these wonderful moments. Expertise and technical skills, many of which I myself don't have, must be brought to bear to improve the lives of disabled people. We don't have to choose between empowering experiences on the one hand and benefiting from rare expertise on the other.

In a fictional account of the relationship between the Cambridge mathematician G.H. Hardy and the self-taught Indian mathematical genius Srinivasa Ramanujan, the novelist David Leavitt has Hardy say this, when reminiscing about his relationship with Ramanujan:

I tried to make a virtue of his ignorance, to persuade myself and others that he profited from the years he spent in isolation, when in fact they were an insurmountable handicap.[2]

I do not believe that all 'handicaps', as Leavitt's character puts it, are insurmountable, but I can understand the pain of the character in wishing that the reality of isolation and difficulty could be removed, and turned into a strength. And I agree that denial of difficult things, however well meant, can be more damaging than recognising them and acknowledging their power.

I write these words with what I hope is cool authority – I feel I am making sense as I make this argument. But when my colleague and I were disagreeing on this issue, I felt anything but cool. I was enraged, far out of proportion to the situation. I think I managed to keep my feelings in check to some degree, as even at the time of our argument I could sense that this difference between my colleague and me had to do with personal issues for me and, I suspected, for her as well. My mode of argument in response to the challenge I'd had from my colleague was also interesting. I am usually quite chatty and humorous in meetings, and I find discussion and debate great fun (I'm lucky to be an academic!). But in this situation I became cold and decisive. I brooked no argument and stated my case forcefully. I had the right to do this, and I don't think I was rude or unfair – I hope not. But my whole way of being in this argument was quite far from my usual facilitative self: I was enacting another role. Irony of ironies, I found myself, this sissy who through ineptitude disrupted the swimming gala at Lichtenburg Primary School, being the ultimate white male in a world of disability and female caring and sharing. I was dominant and forceful and not altogether facilitative. This is not wholly a bad thing; I think it's important that people who have things to say and do, say and do them. But I would be missing something important about that meeting if I overlooked the part that was an enactment in which I certainly participated, and I think my colleague did too.

Disability research, and especially disability research conducted by able-bodied people influenced by the social model, happens at the interface between two different modes of being. On the one hand we have the facilitative, liberation-orientated world of disability politics. On the other we have the competitive world of mastery and dominance of the hard edge of research. As I've mentioned, I've always had trouble accepting the part of me that is indeed the tough researcher – the guy who can get things done, can compete, can get the research grants, can get articles into the prestigious journals. But part of me it is, and I'm glad for it, as it gives me enormous pleasure. I have less trouble accepting the part of me that is the caricature of the psychologist – caring and sharing, helping people find their own way in the world. Both these sides are part of me, and I'm glad I have both sides as part of the way I am in the world. But in the discussion with my colleague, I quickly enacted one side of myself (and of the disability/research divide), just as she, an ambitious and successful woman in her own right, enacted the other. We were playing roles that were comfortably familiar, as it's much easier to think of there being clear divisions between 'empowerment of disabled people' and 'hard-nosed research' than to think of things as being much more fluid. I'm with Tom Shakespeare in his argument that the ideo-logical purity of certain strains of the disability movement, though very helpful in defining and sustaining a political movement, does not provide sufficient grounding for good and vibrant research. And, paradox of paradoxes, when things get difficult and these things need to be discussed, I retreat into the comfortable stereotype of the cold-hearted researcher.

I think all of us involved in disability research, both disabled and able-bodied people, need to recognise that playing these roles scripted by a neatly divided world does everything to reinforce stereotypes and little to move the disability-research agenda forward. My part in contributing to the ongoing splits that operate in the disability-research world links for me very directly to where I started – as the son of a disabled man. I push and shove to do a lot of disability research and to convince people of my views because, for me, the stakes are high and the issues so close to home. This engagement has much to recommend it, but it's also dangerous because my emotional commitment to things can cloud my judgement and make me more strident than I want to be or should be. There are worse things than being personally involved in my work – I wouldn't want it any other way – but there are costs too. I have encountered a rage among some able-bodied research colleagues about the injustices done to disabled people, and I've been on the wrong end of this rage too, which has not been at all pleasant, and has hurt me. This rage is a good thing – it's right to be angry about injustice and oppression, and rage is an appropriate response. But for me, the trick is to channel the rage into useful work and not to be consumed by it. We don't have to be angry on behalf of disabled people – they can be angry all by themselves. What we need to do is to work to use our anger to make things different. Because of my passion for disability issues I get things wrong, and my colleagues do too. But as we think about and process these things, we may get things right more often. The disability movement can benefit from our passion; it does not deserve the baggage that can go with this passion. Does my writing this ensure that I won't load my work with my baggage in the future? Unlikely, alas. But here's to trying.

II

Into Africa

T he flight was fully booked, and there was a carnival atmosphere as we boarded the plane. Passengers carried on bags
of food and household essentials as hand luggage: packets of
mielie meal, sugar and tea; loaves of bread; tinned goods; electronic
equipment; and clothes. It was a bit like being in Checkers Hyper-
market at the end of the month, but the mood was much more
good-humoured, as people chatted away in English, Sindebele and
Shona. It was impossible not to be part of the general conversation
and bustle, and people did not seem to mind sharing space with
mielie meal, blankets and household goods. We were on our way
from Johannesburg to Bulawayo in late 2007, and we all knew that
basic commodities were almost impossible to obtain in Zimbabwe,
as a result of the madnesses of the Mugabe regime. Some of us
– most, it seemed to me – were family members going home,
Zimbabweans lucky enough to have found work in South Africa,
providing an income for their families back home. I was heading
to a meeting with the Southern Africa Federation of the Disabled
(SAFOD), which operates in ten southern African countries and
has its headquarters in Lobengula Street in Bulawayo. I was looking

forward to seeing my SAFOD colleagues, many of whom I'd met previously in other countries, but I was also apprehensive.

I didn't know quite what to expect from Mugabe's Zimbabwe, but I had heard stories about people who brought food into the country being arrested for illegally importing goods. My suitcase was full to bursting with tinned goods, sugar, tea, powdered milk, biscuits and whatever else I could think of that might be useful to people who had no access to everyday basics. As luck would have it, I was one of the people whose bags were opened and checked in the hot, corrugated-iron makeshift airport building. But the customs official was friendly, and perfunctorily looked through the groceries I'd brought and waved me on my way. The SAFOD driver was waiting for me in his familiar vehicle which I'd seen at a recent meeting in Botswana. As we drove through the wide Bulawayo streets to my hotel, he explained why there were so few cars on the road. There was no petrol to be had in Zimbabwe; vehicles that did have fuel, like his, must have been filled up across the Botswana border a four hours' drive away.

My hotel brought back memories of my childhood in what was then Rhodesia – it was a Tudor-style building set in well-tended gardens, with brass and copper ornaments and Dickens prints on the walls. Walking into it was like stepping back into the colonies. The description of the hotel I found on the internet is accurate:

THE CRESTA CHURCHILL HOTEL

Steeped in history, the Tudor charm of the hotel wins over many a traveller. Set in the peaceful, tree-lined streets of Bulawayo, this hotel offers the ideal balance between business and pleasure – capturing true 'old world' comforts.

For the avid bird watcher the Matopos National Park is a must and other natural heritage sites include Victoria Falls and the resting place of Cecil Rhodes.[1]

I was shown from the lobby through the Axminster-carpeted guest lounge to my immaculate room, where I had a few hours' wait until SAFOD were ready for me. The ubiquitous television with South African cable channels (M-Net has truly conquered Africa) was showing an English film of the 'country mystery' type, well loved, I believe, in the USA. The film was beautifully dressed, with interiors not dissimilar to the Cresta Churchill Hotel, and featured gin at sundowners, teas with rock cakes, and the vicar popping in with his humorous wisdom. I had been in Zimbabwe on brief visits since we left in 1966, but this felt like a journey back to the lost world I'd come from. The 'old world comforts' promised by the hotel, in the Zimbabwe of 2007, were clearly 'steeped in (the) history' of the white colonisers and not in the history of liberation. I grew up as a little English boy (or wannabe-English boy, as my family was not English) in what was then Rhodesia, and now, to begin my work with black disabled Zimbabweans, I was back in the Enid Blyton world of the brass horns of the hunt, the vicar coming to tea, and the All's Right With Our Island Empire. That evening I ate supper alone in the hotel dining room, where I was served by men in white uniforms with red sashes. There was something poignant about the whole performance of the meal. I was offered a menu with great flourish, but everything I asked for was not available; there was no milk, no bread, no chicken, no fish. Eventually I asked, 'What *do* you have?' and I was served the only food they had — some rather tough beef. Presenting me with the menu, I came to realise, had nothing to do with offering me alternative foods, but was an indication to me that the staff of the hotel, though they had little to offer in these straitened times, knew what it meant to be hospitable and polite. And that indeed meant something.

As we drove through the streets of suburban and downtown Bulawayo to SAFOD, I saw more of what had become of this colonial city, which I had never known very well as a boy but which had some similarities to the Salisbury of old. The water system in the city had broken down, and most plants, including those in the large gardens, were dead. The red earth showed through the bleached-white grass. Every so often we passed a house that had its own borehole, and there would be the kind of garden I remembered from my boyhood, full of green grass, dahlias, roses and large flowering trees, bright colours everywhere. It was jacaranda season, and I was treated to the sight of enormous canopies of wildly flowering purple blooms. I wondered whether the jacarandas my mother had planted in Salisbury back in 1956 were blooming there as well. The purple flowers were a poignant reminder that the jacaranda is an alien tree, imported by colonists to beautify the local rough terrain. The jacarandas, like the Churchill Hotel, were one of the few things of beauty that remained in the bleak landscape of Mugabe's Zimbabwe.

Having heard of the political oppression in Zimbabwe, I was amazed to see anti-Mugabe slogans on a number of walls and I was surprised by the openness with which my driver discussed the political situation and his opposition to Mugabe (an open discussion which did not cease even when we gave a lift to a uniformed and armed soldier who was forced to hitchhike because the military had no fuel and no working vehicles). As I looked at the city I could see the outlines of the beautiful colonial place it had once been, with its wide tree-lined streets and green parks. I felt guilty at my nostalgia for a time – yes, the 'old world' time of the Churchill Hotel – when privilege was reserved for so few people, when I was part of the race inhabiting and deemed entitled to what was forever England in a corner of Africa, while most Africans were systematically and brutally excluded. I was touched by the shopfront of Meikles, the smartest department store in Bulawayo. There was a display of dozens of bottles of Handy Andy household cleaner, all neatly lined up and beautifully arranged. As far as I could tell, there was nothing else for sale in the shop, and this impression was confirmed by my driver. Outside the banks were long queues of people, patiently waiting to withdraw the small amounts of money they were permitted to take out, in accordance with the ridiculous financial regulations of the country.

The SAFOD offices were very basic but comfortable and friendly, and the people who worked there were clearly used to things taking a long time; they seemed to have a patience which I certainly don't have. One of the major functions of the office was to ensure that everyone who worked for SAFOD had at least one square meal a day, and I was delighted to be offered the free staff lunch of sadza and stew. The SAFOD workers were grateful for the supplies I had brought and inventoried all of them carefully, but I learnt that because SAFOD has overseas funding and a research office in Francistown, just over the border in Botswana, the staff could access supplies from there. There had been a plan to move the entire office to Francistown, but because of immigration problems SAFOD has remained in Bulawayo. Zimbabwe (and Bulawayo in particular) has a proud history regarding services for disabled people; the Jairos Jiri Association, which was established in the 1950s, has been a long-standing champion of disability rights. Hospitable and calm, the SAFOD staff members were articulate and pragmatic in their discussions about the work they were doing, about what they could and couldn't do, and about their constant battles to do good in the context of the brutality of the Mugabe regime.

I was impressed as ever with the quick intelligence and political savvy of Alexander Phiri, the director-general of SAFOD. I had already met him a few times, but it was good to see him in the relaxed atmosphere of his own office, and he chatted with me about our work together and, with great frankness, about other matters. 'People tell me,' he said, 'that you're all a lot of white racists at Stellenbosch, and that we shouldn't work with you.' I was able to discuss in some detail with Alexander where I thought this kind of allegation came from, the basis it did have in historical fact, how Stellenbosch has a long way to go in terms of race issues, but how, at the same time, there is much good at Stellenbosch, and how happy I am to be there. Alexander listened with his usual good-humoured attention, and I think he was more than slightly amused to see me squirm a bit as I tried to defend my decision to be at Stellenbosch. After I'd given my explanation, in which I neither apologised for nor dissociated myself from Stellenbosch, Alexander said he was satisfied with what I'd said. 'I take people as I find them,' he told me, and I believe him. He is a person who respects others and who knows his own mind.

Some months later, when our work with SAFOD was well

under way, Alexander and his team from the SAFOD leadership came to visit us at Stellenbosch. The visit was not altogether easy for Lehlohonolo Mafofo, chairperson of SAFOD and based in Lesotho. He told me that many years before he had applied to study medicine at the university, but had been told that his application would not be considered because he is disabled (he has a mobility impairment, but I can see no reason why this should have prevented him from becoming a medical doctor). I hope that the good experience we had together went some way to restoring good relationships between the university and Lehlohonolo.

A highlight of the visit was a lecture Alexander gave to my students. Alexander is an articulate and charismatic man, and my students, most of whom were white South Africans with little exposure to the world of disability in our country or in Africa, sat in rapt attention. Alexander told of how he had been disabled as a young boy. His legs had been cut off in a motor vehicle accident. He had gone to hospital, and his family, who were poor labourers, had left him there and vanished without a trace. They were obviously worried about the burden a child with a substantial physical impairment would be to the family, so they had abandoned him to his fate. 'Becoming disabled,' Alexander said, 'was the best thing that ever happened to me.' In hospital he was looked after by a nurse who was out from England for a short stay, working in what was then Rhodesia. Not surprisingly, given Alexander's personality, this little abandoned boy found his way into the nurse's heart. She decided to stay on in Rhodesia and brought him up as her own child. Alexander completed schooling and tertiary education, and has become an internationally known and respected figure in the disability movement. All this, he says, would have been highly unlikely had he not been disabled – he would probably not have had much schooling and, if he were lucky, would have found work as a peasant labourer. Given the life expectancy in Zimbabwe among poor people in particular, he might well have died young had he not been disabled. The most remarkable part of Alexander's story, though, is that when he became well known, his mother came looking for him (his father had since passed away), asking him to help the family financially. A lesser person would, with justification, have turned away the family that had abandoned him. But in a gesture which has echoes in the biblical story of Joseph meeting his brothers after they left him for dead, Alexander was able to embrace his family again. He had a house built for his mother and remains in touch with her.

Not surprisingly, this story moved my students and me very deeply, but this was not all there was in Alexander's lecture. About two-thirds of the way through his talk, his cellphone rang. Only Alexander could get away with what happened next. He answered the phone and, while we all watched and waited, he made arrangements with a Japanese colleague about an upcoming visit he was making to Japan. He took it in good humour when I teased him in front of the students, saying that I believed he had prearranged the call just so he could show us what a big shot he is internationally. The students were indeed impressed with Alexander's international status being enacted in front of them, and the whole visit was, I think, a great success. This was notwithstanding my embarrassment that, apart from the ground floor, the building in which I work is not accessible to wheelchair users, despite repeated complaints from me and my colleagues. As of writing, the building remains inaccessible, and it is discomfiting that I was able to welcome my SAFOD friends to Stellenbosch but not into my office. Obviously we still have some way to go.

Along with several colleagues, I have the daunting task of providing research training and consultation services to SAFOD members. This is a wonderful project which I'm lucky to be part of, and I've learnt a lot through my work with SAFOD about what successful disability activism is. It's sometimes much quieter than one would imagine. For example, we once held a workshop in a hotel in Gaborone, and it was difficult for wheelchair users to get into the room where we were working. There was no fuss, no loud protesting, but by the second day of our meeting, the SAFOD leadership had had a quiet word with the hotel management and a ramp was being built while we were still there. At a meeting at a hotel in Maputo, Alexander pointed out to me all the accessible features of the hotel. He and SAFOD had been using the hotel for years and had persuaded the management to make these changes. In a context in which there is very little accommodation for disabled people, these small victories have a significance that goes beyond the local scale on which they happen. It's not all victory, of course. I knew in theory and had seen instances on a small scale of how disabled people can be disregarded and discriminated against in public spaces, but I was appalled to see how my SAFOD colleagues were treated at Gaborone airport after a workshop. My Stellenbosch colleague Melanie Basson and I were the only two white people in our party leaving Gaborone at a particular time, and we were also the only two people from the workshop who had no visible impairments. The airport staff, clearly overwhelmed by the large number of people arriving with wheelchairs and crutches, and others who were blind, were uniformly rude to their customers. All conversation was directed to Melanie or me, despite our pointing out that wheelchair users and blind people are quite capable of answering for themselves. The staff seemed angry, and we were offered no help in assisting our colleagues through customs and security. I am anxious in airports at the best of times, and am always convinced I am going to miss my plane. Trying to shepherd two blind people and three wheelchair users simultaneously through a circuitous security path did little to calm my nerves. I did see the funny side, though, when a customs official simply refused to believe that he could not get a blind colleague to read and sign a customs declaration on his own. When I pointed out that my colleague could not see, the official took stock of the situation and, in a very loud, very slow voice, repeated his instructions that my colleague must read and fill in the form. This was the one occasion in the airport when an official had actually engaged with and spoken directly to a disabled person, and there was something tragicomic about the fact that this potentially empowering moment was based on a gross misunderstanding of what this person's impairment was. I suppose the official's personal philosophy was something that was being tested that day: 'There's none so blind as those who will not see,' he seemed to believe.

Working with SAFOD on building research capacity has been and continues to be an enriching experience for me. When Melanie and I were preparing a participatory research training workshop, for example, we found that almost all good participatory learning techniques depend on people having vision. All the handbooks and websites have community members sitting around (some in wheelchairs) drawing things, making maps, sticking things on walls or trees, taking photographs with disposable cameras. We decided to use some community mapping techniques, but made special allowances for people who were blind or had severe visual impairments to do modified exercises which made use of verbal rather than visual skills. After the exercise was complete and we were discussing it in the larger group, one of the blind participants said, 'Don't be so sure that blind people don't know about what places look like. In fact, we are the best geographers.' The other blind participants immediately knew what he meant. They pointed out that they all live in inhospitable environments, where there is poor road upkeep, where traffic is heavy and often very fast, where there are no pedestrian crossings that indicate it is safe to walk by the sounding of a bell, where people live and trade on pavements which were designed for pedestrians but no longer serve that function, or they live in rural areas where there are no tarred roads and it can be muddy, with pathways barely accessible. As a result of this, they are acutely aware of the physical environment, of how many steps it takes to go here or there, of road surfaces changing, of where it is (comparatively) safe to cross a road. The blind participants were amused to tell the rest of the group that whenever they get together, they discuss the physical environment in great detail, and therefore they know more about what places look like than the rest of us do![2] The wonderful thing about this revelation to all the sighted people in the room was that it was one of those moments of complete inversion – a moment in which we realise that something we had thought of only as a problem or even a weakness turns out to be quite a strength.

Working with SAFOD has also caused me to revisit some of the powerful insights in Valerie Sinason's book *Mental Handicap and the Human Condition*.[3] In this book, she develops the idea of what she terms 'secondary handicap'[4] – the way in which people with disabilities (she's interested specifically in intellectual disability, but her argument has implications more broadly) may exaggerate their impairments and difficulties in response to the oppressive world around them. She gives some moving examples of how people exaggerate what they can't do, and how, in a respectful and healing environment, they come to reclaim capacity they have always had. Valerie's work draws deeply on psychoanalytic theory but is also in perfect tune with what disability theorists have long argued: that disability is not just a matter of impairment, but is also a matter of how disabled people are treated in the world. With her nuanced understanding of trauma and its effects, she shows how disabled people – like many oppressed people everywhere – can take on and even participate in their own oppression, as the only familiar emotional space for them is a space within which they are vilified and humiliated.

In contrast to the people Valerie sees in her clinical practice, the people I work with in SAFOD are generally very successful people who have done well in their lives despite the difficulties they face in their communities and their countries. They are also a diverse group with respect to formal training – in one group we had someone who was finishing off a doctorate together with people who had not completed high school. I'm not sure what I expected when I began training with this mixed group, but something became clear very quickly. As we began to discuss research principles with them, they grasped quite readily the idea that researchers should take nothing for granted, that they should see the world as strange, that they should accept nothing at face value. This ability to 'make strange', as the anthropologists put it, does not come at all easily to many of my graduate students, including students who do very well academically. But here were people, many of whom have no research training at all, who had an immediate feel for a core quality of a good researcher – the ability to look beyond the obvious.

As I thought about this and discussed this issue with participants, I suddenly realised that there may be another side to the 'secondary handicap' story. Just as many people under difficult circumstances and oppression may develop secondary handicap, there may also be those disabled people who, like psychologists, develop the kind of research-mindedness I described in the previous chapter. If you look or sound different from other people and you are subjected to various forms of discrimination throughout life, but you have good internal resources (which may come from a good family start in life), then what do you do? Talking to my SAFOD friends, I've come to realise that one of the things that can happen if you grow up disabled is that you learn to watch the world very closely – to see the world as strange. Being different and being judged for being different may crush some people, but for others it may lead to a heightened ability to question things, to ask why, not to accept – in a nutshell, to become a natural researcher.

I worry as I write this that my comments may be misread, as they may appear moralistic or elitist: 'bad' disabled people develop secondary handicap; 'good' disabled people develop research abilities. This would clearly be nonsense, and would be another form of blaming disabled people who do not do well for their oppression. But when we think about 'subjugated knowledges' and what disabled people know already, it's helpful if we give more thought not just to what disabled people may know already, but also to the processes by which they come to know things. That is, we need to learn more about what marginality and oppression can do to how we think about the world. This is quite a tall order, and I suspect things are much more complex than 'secondary handicap' on the one hand and 'research-mindedness' on the other, but I'm looking forward to discovering more about these issues. I'm learning so much through my work with disabled people, and I hope what I'm discussing here will show not that I mean this in a mealy-mouthed politically correct way (we all have to say we learn from the 'other'), but that it reflects my experience of being forced to think about things, including about what my bread and butter – research – really is.

I've learnt some other things along the way too. Whenever I am working with disabled colleagues from other African countries, somebody will either tease me or engage with me quite seriously about South African politics and South African disability politics in particular. People have said to me that South Africans are difficult and doctrinaire, rigid on principles and less than facilitative in practice. I am never quite sure what to make of these discussions. Part of me feels very defensive – it's inevitable that the regional power which is so much richer than any of the surrounding countries should be envied and criticised by others. But if I am to be honest, I don't think this is the whole story. On one memorable occasion a colleague from another country said, with a mixture of humour and irritation, 'Come now, Leslie, stop trying

so hard to say and do the right thing – you're among friends.' He
had a point. I'm so aware of the politics of disability research and
of racial politics that I do sometimes try too hard to be sensitive
to the power issues at stake. To my African colleague, though, it
was more important that I relax, offer what I have to offer and stop
worrying about things that are accepted among us. I do not have
to keep proving my bona fides. I think it's true that South Africans
have some way to go to feel that we can trust one another and,
more importantly in some ways, that we can trust others to trust
us. This has been a valuable lesson for me from my more relaxed
colleagues from other countries.

I've also thought a lot in the context of my work about what
in South Africa is known as *ubuntu*, or 'humanness'. The fundamental principle of *ubuntu* is that we are human through our
interconnectedness, through mutuality of give and take, and
through caring for one another. My colleague Gubela Mji and her
collaborators have done some important and path-breaking work
on developing an African disability-research network, which they
call the African Network for Evidence-to-Action on Disability
(AfriNEAD). They argue that central to establishing this network
has been working in accordance with *ubuntu* principles.[5] When
I see how Gubela and her colleagues work, I don't have any
problem recognising *ubuntu* in action, but I have long been quite
cynical about the use of this term in South Africa, which is such
a violent country and one in which many human networks have
broken down. I see politicians who are selfish and corrupt justify-
ing their own selfish actions with reference to *ubuntu*. But when
I think about how I have been accepted and allowed to offer what
I have to offer to many friends and colleagues in the disability

movement both in South Africa and beyond, and the chances I've been given to learn, I start to think (somewhat to my embarrassment) that there may be something to this *ubuntu* thing after all. It's not just a South African concept (in Malawi, for example, it's known as *umunthu*), and it does seem to me that mutuality, the ability to both give and receive, is important, especially to the operation of organisations like SAFOD. There are, of course, corresponding non-African ways of describing how we work. It's useful, for example, to think of doing research work in community organisations or disabled people's organisations in terms of the concept of developing a 'community of practice'.[6] But, sentimental or not, I like to think that there's indeed something quintessentially African about these developing research networks. For me, the chance to go back and rework some of my colonial Rhodesian boyhood is a wonderful opportunity – a gift. I have been given, and have taken, a chance to do something which I hope will help disabled people. In a small but personally important way, I have also been able to help redress some of the imbalances in access to knowledge and skills, access which provided me with education and privilege that I inherited rather than earned. Through the generosity of others I am allowed both to enjoy my privilege and to use it to try to make things better.

12

Home

In 2006 my colleagues and I were fortunate to launch our
book *Disability and Social Change: A South African Agenda*[1]
at a meeting organised by the publishers in the old women's jail
at the Constitutional Court in Johannesburg. My daughters, Alison
and Rebecca, and I drove up from Cape Town by car (Louise flew
to Johannesburg, as long car trips were difficult because of her
hip). The N1 passes very near the town of Hennenman and near
White's, where my father managed the cement factory for a few
years in the late 1960s and early 1970s. I decided to take a detour
to show Alison and Rebecca my old house.

We found Hennenman without difficulty, and it was much
more prosperous than I had anticipated – in this Free State dorp
there was even a Pick n Pay mini market. The one women's
clothing store – Die Mode – was gone, but I was able to point out
to the girls the location of the two men's clothing stores which
were a block apart and had both been owned by the Isaacson
family. One shop had been for whites and the other, a shabbier
and dingier shop, had been for blacks. I was sad but not surprised
to see that the Dukas Café was no longer in business, though its

curving glass shopfront was still there. Before the days of Pick n Pay and the Spar, when we lived in White's we would go for supplies to the Dukas Café. During the long holidays when I was home from boarding school, my mother would buy me ice lollies while she chatted with Mrs Dukas and bought what she needed. Mrs Dukas was always pleasant, and habitually punctuated her conversations with customers with the question 'And what else?' as she bustled backwards and forwards behind the counter, assembling what people needed and chatting all the while. As long as my hands were clean and not too sticky with ice lolly, Mrs Dukas didn't mind if I quickly thumbed through the comics and picture books stacked on racks at the front of the shop. We often ended up buying something, such as a *Personality* magazine or *Darling* for my sister. Superman comics, so much part of my childhood, were already hard to find in those days. Though my rational mind tells me that I must have bought the special black-and-white souvenir copy of *Scope* which commemorated the first heart transplant in 1967, before we moved to the Free State in 1968, my memory places me buying that *Scope* magazine from Mrs Dukas. *And* what else?

We drove on through Hennenman, and found that the hotel where commercial travellers had stayed and where my father went to Rotary meetings was now derelict. The hairdresser across the way from the hotel, where every Saturday morning my mother had sat with her hair in rollers, was also gone. We had some trouble finding White's, the cement factory and little village where white workers at the factory had lived (black workers were in inferior quarters across the railway line), but eventually the familiar display wall with the blue circle came into view. We turned right into the housing estate, skirted a large puddle of water, and were on our way to Portland House, where our family had lived almost forty years ago.

Portland House was certainly the grandest house we had ever lived in. Not too long after the brothers Mr White and Mr White came out to South Africa to establish a cement factory on the rich limestone deposit in what was then the Orange Free State, the housing estate for cement factory staff was laid out, with Portland House, the cement factory manager's house, as its centrepiece. A Herbert Baker–style building (we could never establish whether Herbert Baker, the famous architect, designed the house himself or whether it was a knock-off), it had Cape Dutch gables, and was imposingly arranged around a large open courtyard. Access to the house was via a sweeping drive which went around the house, and the grand gates of Portland House could be seen from quite a way off. Portland House was of far smarter and more opulent style than the more modest homes around it, and was clearly an expression by the White's Cement Company of what it aspired to be. The first time I saw Portland House was when we visited it after my father heard that he was to be promoted from deputy manager at Lichtenburg to manager of the White's works. We drove up the drive in our much-hated company Wolseley, and, hot and sticky from the long journey, we were invited in for tea. Three adolescent boys, all older than me, were sprawled on the floor reading magazines. These brothers had lived here for some time and their father, like mine, had recently been promoted, and was off to work at the head office in Johannesburg. The boys' mother told them to show me around the house (my sister was still away at school), but for what felt like forever they did not give any sign that they had noticed me or heard their mother. Eventually I was grudgingly shown around the impressive house with its four bedrooms and two bathrooms and large garden, well tended by gardeners provided by the factory.

Not long after that we moved in, and my sister and I would live there during school holidays. The move to the Free State was far less of a shock than the move from Salisbury to Lichtenburg had been, and the atmosphere in the Free State, contrary to our expectations, was far less harsh than that in Lichtenburg. We felt that we were less in the right-wing heartland than we had been in Lichtenburg, which was important for a liberal Jewish family. Years later, when the white right wing threatened to destabilise the transition to democracy in South Africa, we were not surprised that its power base was concentrated in the Lichtenburg area, and that when former president F.W. de Klerk asked white South Africans in a referendum whether they supported his reforms, the Free State went with most of the country in supporting them, while the Lichtenburg area opposed them. We were, I think, quite happy in Portland House. I had some friends, Jewish boys, in Hennenman, but mostly I spent my holidays at Portland House reading, huddled for warmth against the severe Free State cold, and playing in the garden, including terrorising the goldfish in the pond, trying to catch them in a makeshift net I fashioned from a wire coat hanger and my mother's old pantyhose. On one occasion only did I catch a goldfish. I put it in water in the bath inside the house, watched it flop about unhappily for a few minutes and then returned it to the pond.

When Alison, Rebecca and I arrived at White's, I had not been back there for well over thirty years, and I had told the girls something of what had been an illustrious chapter in the Swartz family history. But the housing estate had changed dramatically, and I think the factory had long since closed down. Houses previously inhabited by white families and serviced by black servants were now home to black people. Many of the flower gardens were now flourishing vegetable gardens, with bright green mielie plants shining in the Free State sun. We drove up to Portland House and saw immediately that it was an uninhabited ruin. The majestic gateway to the now broken-down driveway was inexpertly but effectively criss-crossed with wire, so we parked outside the property, gingerly stepped over the crumbling low garden wall and went to look at what remained of the house. The most obvious ruin, apart from the house itself, was the large tiled hole of the swimming pool, and I hastened to tell the girls that the pool had been added only after we had left White's. We entered part of the ruin of the house, which by now had no roof and had been stripped bare of every wall tile, every bath and basin, and every useful piece of piping. There was graffiti on the walls, including the usual sexual drawings and some swastikas. The wooden floors were gone, and in order to get around the house we had to step on broken roof tiles. We did not go into every room, but I stopped in what had been my parents' room, where for some reason I remembered with great clarity having sat on the edge of their bed in 1969 listening to the broadcast of Neil Armstrong setting foot on the moon. That July was bitterly cold in the Free State and Portland House was poorly heated, so we shivered as we listened and drank our tea, with me thinking partly of men on the moon and partly about the impending end of the winter holidays and the return to boarding school.

Alison and Rebecca were upset about the state of my old home, and I wished I could have spared them this, but at the time I personally felt strangely unmoved. I noticed that with the garden now all long dead, it was possible to look out along the flat and beautiful Free State plains, a view we had never had when surrounded by a garden with exotic plants like pomegranate trees and large rose bushes. There was a discolouration in the grass where the fish pond had been, and only a single wall remained of the servants' quarters, where our maid Anna Mothupi had lived and where she had given birth to her two sons, Peter and Alfred, Alfred having been named after my father. We made our way back to the car, and suddenly I felt the urge to get away and back on the highway to Johannesburg.

Just as we were about to drive off, a man appeared seemingly from nowhere and began to tell us what he knew of the history of the house. He said that when the houses in the estate had been sold off, most had sold for under R40 000 but this big house had sold for R60 000 (if the house had been situated in Cape Town it would probably have sold for at least R3 million). The people who had bought the house had not been able to keep up the payments and had left in the dead of night. Nobody else could afford the house, and eventually children had started bashing the house down and vandalising it. He said this with a sort of resigned sadness, and the whole moment of his being there to tell us this story had for me a Dickensian quality to it – I felt like Pip returning to where he had first seen Magwitch and finding an elderly man from the country waiting there to tell him the story of what had happened to his past. My informant was clearly poor, but he did not ask for money. Instead he told me about the lack of jobs in the area and asked if I knew anyone who could establish a BJ's there (a petrol station with fast-food restaurant and convenience store attached, such as are found on all major roads in South Africa). This, he said, would bring in jobs, and would do well, as lots of cars passed between Hennenman and White's. Sadly, on this issue I disagreed with him, but did not say so. I shook his hand and pressed some money in to it, and we drove on.

We went past the other houses of the estate, most of them in reasonable repair, and along to White's golf course, which was still very well maintained. There were large German cars parked outside the clubhouse, and some white people could be seen playing on the links. Some things don't change. One of the biggest controversies of my father's tenure as factory manager and de facto mayor of White's housing estate was when he organised a golf day for all the caddies who carried people's clubs around the nine holes. Some of the caddies were gifted golfers, but not all the burghers of White's and the surrounding towns and farms felt ready for black people playing on their course and with their clubs. Others were angry that the caddies' day was on a Sunday, the Lord's day, but my father knew that had he interfered with white people's golf on any other day (it was unthinkable that black and white people could share a course on the same day) he would have had a lynching on his hands.

I wondered why Alison and Rebecca were more upset than I was at the state of the house where I had once lived but which they had never seen, and which was situated in a world completely apart from the urban Cape Town of their lives. Part of my calm, I knew, resulted from the fact that despite the reality that the girls were now grown women – Alison nearly twenty and

Rebecca nearly eighteen – as their father, I wanted to be calm and to protect them from upset. Not such a bad thing. But as I thought about it in the months that followed and retold the story over and over again, I came to believe that there was something else to my muted reaction.

I thought of the three large boys whom I'd seen on my first visit to Portland House, and their sense of ownership of the place. I thought of my mother's upset at being told by the manager's wife who had moved into the house after us, 'We've had a nice glass covering put over the central courtyard of the house, which makes it much cosier. And we've put in a pool. Isn't it nice that every manager's wife is allowed to do something to fix up the house to her liking? We were so lucky to get to have two things fixed up.' My mother was polite but quietly furious – she had never asked for, had never been offered, had never been given any changes to Portland House. Though she had found the building beautiful, she experienced the house as very cold, and she had fretted over the fact that visitors from the London office would notice that we could not afford a carpet for the large and freezing dining room. My parents – my father in particular – had rather liked the grandness of the house, but if the truth be told, they had never really settled there. They had perched in these large baronial rooms on their comfortable but comparatively spindly fifties-style furniture, their only indulgence being a gold Dralon lounge suite. They were uncomfortable in the house but could not ask for it to be made more comfortable. I understand that in contemporary architecture there is now a fondness for designing buildings that 'tread lightly on the earth'; it feels to me that in that world of cement and concrete, in a house that was energy-inefficient and the opposite of 'green', my parents 'trod lightly' in the house. They passed through not as temporary owners of the place but as sojourners, wandering Jews.

Part of this came from their having spent much of their married life in company housing (until my father was forty-nine and we moved to the head office in Johannesburg), in common with many other people who worked at cement factories or on mines, but I think other people who were also in company housing had a different approach. Our neighbours in Salisbury kept changing and adding to their company house, something they felt was their due as he was factory manager (as my father was at White's), and by the time we left Salisbury their standard-issue fifties bungalow had been transformed into a double storey complete with arches and niches to accommodate the religious icons and crucifixes they liked to display. My father was scrupulously opposed to anything that smacked remotely of corruption and of using company resources for personal ends, and this is part of the story but not all of it. My father, the only Jew in the company internationally, always felt out of place, and so did my mother. Did my dad's physical impairment have anything to do with this? I don't know, but for me it was part of what made him (and us) different from the families all around us – the teenage boys lolling around Portland House when we went to see our new home, and those who came after us and were given a swimming pool.

After my strange and unexpected return to Portland House, while in Johannesburg I decided to visit the houses we had lived in there, the only two houses my father ever owned. Our little house in Highlands North, where I'd lived on the sun porch because we did not have enough bedrooms and my grandmother was living with us and needed a room of her own, was now bolted and barred against criminals and intruders, making the house a quintessentially contemporary Johannesburg residence/fortress. It revealed nothing to me as I drove by. Neither did the house we had moved into in Parktown North as my father moved rapidly up in the world – the driveway of the panhandled stand was now firmly blocked by a (very attractive) garage door. No luck with either visit. So I tried to think about what for me were defining moments of our lives in each house.

For the first house, the moment was in a sense so predictable as to be laughable. I have a vivid memory of my mother finally losing her temper at my grandmother's goading one morning in the kitchen and calling Granny an ignoramus. 'Igmaramus!' shouted Granny in response. 'Igmaramus! You have the cheek to call me an igmaramus!' Things then became too much for Granny, enraged as she was. She was forced to take out her false teeth and she put them down on the kitchen table. She then pounded the table repeatedly, and I can still see her teeth bouncing around each time she hit the table and simultaneously shouted through flaccid lips, 'Igmaramus! Igmaramus!'

I have two core memories of the bigger house in Parktown North, and again the first is predictable. Weekends in that house tended to be rather busy, as on occasion we would have staying with us Granny, Auntie Lea, and my mother's sister Auntie Tilly (she who had nicknamed Lea the Buchenwald Chicken). Thin though Auntie Lea was, she still felt squashed out of place by the presence of sweet, kind Auntie Tilly, a matter she felt compelled to take into her own hands. 'Why on earth are you here so often,

Tilly?' demanded my father's aunt of my mother's sister. 'After all, Tilly, you're not a close relative.' No problems with a sense of ownership there, or of who was owned by whom.

My second memory of the Parktown North house is much more painful. One day a water mains burst near our house. Water gushed out all over the pavement and down the street. My mother had phoned the municipality and workers were dispatched to the scene when my father, battered by a bad day at work, came home. He raged and raged at this broken pipe, unable to stop himself from blaming everyone for this disaster. I felt frightened of and distant from him at that moment. He seemed so big and so small at the same time.

In some ways this scene sums it all up for me. My father, this brave, brave man who had successfully taken on the world, determined not to be defined by his funny broken body, driving home to his lovely house in his beautiful blue Jaguar. And at the same time, a man who knew what it meant to be hurt and humiliated and who sometimes (not always, not nearly always) just couldn't take it any more. And the morning after his appalling behaviour with the gushing water pipe, he would smile, pick himself up, ignore as far as he could his mother's incessant demands for attention, and start all over again. Such a simple thing, really, but a lesson for my lifetime. Bruised, bloodied, battered, bowed – none of these things are to be ashamed of. Just keep going.

And when I ponder the eccentric course my life has taken, I think it has a lot to do with what I learnt from this man who was in some ways a stranger to me when he died but is still, and more than ever, part of me. At seventeen I found the strength to leave home to make a new life for myself in Cape Town (my father supported me absolutely in this, though it was difficult for my mother to let me go). But in Cape Town I have stayed, an anomaly in the shifting world of my migrating family members, my class-mates, my friends. I've lived in the same house for over twenty years, much longer than my mother lived in any house, and much of this book has been written in my purple and green kitchen (it looks better than it sounds, trust me), where I can look out with pleasure at the unfinished backyard (we ran out of renovation money but hope to have a small fountain there one day). I wouldn't by choice have ended my happy first marriage, but I'm glad the break happened, as this brought me to Louise, without whom many things wouldn't have come about, including this book. I have two remarkable children whom I adore, who are substantial and thoughtful young women.

In so many ways, my life looks and feels like a picture of settled contentment, conventional domesticity, and it is indeed all that, something I am so grateful for and can't quite believe I deserve. But I'm also determinedly, joyfully, nuts. For much of my life I have been fascinated with the subjunctive mode, with the sense in life of 'as if'. Much of this comes from my parents: my mother's mad (and wonderful) choice to marry and love her cripple; and my father's ability, with his intellect and compassion, to be both a success and a kind and good person. I don't think they ever quite felt that they belonged, that they had a home, that they had a life of their own, but somehow within that they made a marriage of, cliché or no cliché, true minds. They struggled and they loved. And writing this book has helped me realise some-thing else. If much of my adult life has been an attempt to live as if I had not been so cut off from my father, so far away from him when he died, I also know that there was something special, something precious he gave me across that gulf that allowed me, compelled me, to do this – to claim back from the world of the subjunctive one of the most important relationships of my life. I loved him and he loved me and the rest, as they say, is detail.

When to my amazement, and following a confluence of circumstances I would never have predicted, I ended up working at Stellenbosch University, I began my inaugural lecture with the question, 'What's a nice Jewish boy doing in a place like this?' Though I cringe a bit at how provocative I was being with that foundation joke for my time in the university, in some senses it's a question I've been asking and will keep asking all my life. I'm all too aware of the Jewish joke, rather dated now, but spot on for my generation: 'What is the definition of a lawyer? A nice Jewish boy who can't stand the sight of blood.' Through some crazy happenstance – which was not happenstance at all – I could not, would not, will not inhabit the usual world of the nice Jewish boy. I can't prove it, but I feel in my bones that this has everything to do with my father's life with his funny body, always an outsider, always out of place, but always, in another way, just himself.

And who would have thought, when it comes to my work life, that I feel at home – yes, at home – in an institution in which Jews are very thin on the ground, a place in which a colleague can tell me without malice, rancour or irony that some of his best friends are Jews, a university which still doesn't seem to get it that it matters, it matters a great deal, that our building is not accessible to disabled people (maybe this book will make a difference – who knows?). At Stellenbosch I happily speak a lot of Afrikaans, though I despair of the language politics which, no matter how you look at it, play a major part in keeping the place far too white. I love the challenge and the joy of trying to talk in and across two languages, and I marvel that it was possible at Stellenbosch for the staff of the department of psychology, a department with a history intertwined with H.F. Verwoerd, to take Xhosa lessons together and to think about our place in South Africa today and in the big new world. And there has also been something marvellous for me in finding a home in a place where, in the words of our visionary former rector, Chris Brink, long since gone from the university, *'Mense is baie gasvry op Stellenbosch maar jy bly nog steeds 'n gas'* (people are very hospitable at Stellenbosch but you still remain a guest). I feel at Stellenbosch so much a sojourner, a guest, a traveller being permitted to pass through, but this, given my life and my history, is precisely what makes me feel at home. And it's because I came to this place and was accepted in this place for who and what I am, nuttiness and all, that I could open my working life to the possibility of disability studies, a decision which at times has hurt like hell but has changed my life for the better. I'm everywhere I shouldn't be in my mad and lovely life. And this is all it really is – crawling, running, hurtling, pushing, shoving, on my way back, back, back, and forward, forward, forward, all the way to you, Dad, to you.

Acknowledgements

This book has been a long time coming. More people were cajoled to read bits or all of it, to give advice and support, to help me along the way, to put up with my despair at various points, than is really decent. Thanks are due to all the following people, each of whom helped in a different way: Adam Alter, Jenny Alter, Rita Barnard, Art Bochner, Vivienne Bozalek, Stine Braathen, Pam Britt, Ronelle Carolissen, Bev Dickman, Tessa Dowling, Susan Filtane, Lisbet Grut, Ashraf Kagee, Dina Katz, Antjie Krog, Brenda Leibowitz, Lehlohonolo Mafofo, Russell Martin, Lindsey Nicholls, Alexander Phiri, Poul Rohleder, Margie Schneider, Tom Shakespeare, Valerie Sinason, Sandra Swart, Mark Tomlinson, Amelia van der Merwe, Hester van der Walt, Brian Watermeyer and Stephen Watson. My Community, Self and Identity research group (Brenda, Lindsey, Poul, Ronelle and Vivienne) have been a consistently supportive team. I am also grateful to Robin Buck and my fellow Fitness Bootcampers for helping keep my insanity at productive levels and for putting more ability into this old body than I thought possible.

Without Mike Nicol's enthusiastic and generous reading of the manuscript, this book might never have found a publisher.

It has been a pleasure working with Robert Plummer, Marlene Fryer and Rashieda Saliem at Zebra Press, and I thank them for their willingness to take a risk with this project and for making the journey so pleasant. Lisa Compton edited the first book I ever published and it was a delight to work with her again.

Stellenbosch University was very generous in giving me study leave, some of which I used for writing this book. I am indebted to all my colleagues and students at Stellenbosch and all the other places I have worked for helping me think about the issues I discuss in this book. My work with SAFOD, the Southern Africa Federation of the Disabled, deserves special mention in this regard: both the trainees and the staff of SAFOD have taught me far more than I have taught them. The SAFOD work, like much of the other work I discuss in this book, was generously funded by various donors, and in this regard I should particularly like to thank the UK Department for International Development (DFID), Save the Children Sweden, the National Research Foundation (South Africa), the Norwegian Research Council, the HSRC, the Royal Netherlands Embassy and the Seventh Framework Programme of the European Union for support for work I've been involved in over the years. None of them funded (or was asked to fund) the writing of this book directly, but all gave me opportunities to do work I've learnt from. It goes without saying of course that any opinions I express in this book are mine alone, and not those of Stellenbosch University or of any funder.

Although I have said throughout this book that all the work I do is driven in no small measure by the most personal of motives, this is the most explicitly personal book I have written. I could not have done this without the love and support of my family. My wife, Louise Frenkel, sat night after night with me listening to me read through drafts, and, even more than this, gave me the courage to take the risk that even starting this book involved. It is no exaggeration to say that without Louise's love, support and careful feedback, much of it given at a time during which she had to face the very painful death of her mother, I would not have been able to write this book. I am a lucky man. My daughters, Alison Swartz and Rebecca Swartz, have helped me along the journey with a generosity and joy that is truly remarkable. And my mother Elsie Swartz has shown a pleasure in and encouragement of this project from the moment she read the draft I shared with her, which reinforces my pride in and admiration for her, especially at a time when her own health is not good.

I wrote this book in memory of my father, and the process has indeed made me feel closer to him than I have ever been aware of before. But it has also reminded me of what my living family gives to me. This book was intended to repay a debt of gratitude to a man long dead. The test of this repayment will be in what it means for those who live on.

LESLIE SWARTZ
CAPE TOWN
FEBRUARY 2010

Notes

CHAPTER 2

1 For an excellent discussion of the history of psychiatry and of family-blaming, especially in the case of autism, see Roy Richard Grinker, *Unstrange Minds: Remapping the World of Autism* (New York: Basic Books, 2007).
2 For a lively history and critique of the social model, see Tom Shakespeare, *Disability Rights and Wrongs* (London: Routledge, 2006).

CHAPTER 3

1 For a more detailed discussion of this, see Leslie Swartz, *Culture and Mental Health: A Southern African View* (Cape Town: Oxford University Press, 1998), especially Chapter 5.
2 See Victoria Nokwanele Mgwili and Brian Watermeyer, 'Physically Disabled Women and Reproductive Health Care: Some Psychoanalytic Reflections on Experiences of Discrimination', in Brian Watermeyer, Leslie Swartz, Theresa Lorenzo, Marguerite Schneider and Mark Priestley (eds), *Disability and Social Change: A South African Agenda* (Cape Town: HSRC Press, 2006), pp. 261–272.
3 See, for example, Judy McKenzie and Bronwyn Müller, 'Parents and Therapists: Dilemmas in Partnership', ibid., pp. 311–323; and Ari Seirlis and Leslie Swartz, 'Entrepreneurship, Employment and Skills Development: Ari Seirlis in Conversation', ibid., pp. 361–372.

4 Valerie Sinason, *Mental Handicap and the Human Condition: New Approaches from the Tavistock* (London: Free Association Press, 1993).

CHAPTER 4

1 See Tom Shakespeare, 'Cultural Representations of Disabled People: Dustbins for Disavowal?', *Disability and Society* 9 (3), 1994, pp. 283–299.
2 For more detail on this, see Leslie Swartz, *Culture and Mental Health: A Southern African View* (Cape Town: Oxford University Press, 1998).
3 Hester van der Walt, 'Too Close for Comfort: Emotional Ties between Nurses and Patients', in Leslie Swartz, Kerry Gibson and Tamara Gelman (eds), *Reflective Practice: Psychodynamic Ideas in the Community* (Cape Town: HSRC Press, 2002), pp. 73–83.

CHAPTER 5

1 Quoted in Brian Raftopolous and Jean-Paul Lacoste, 'Savings Mobilisation to Micro-Finance: A Historical Perspective on the Zimbabwe Savings Development Movement'. Paper presented at the International Conference on Livelihood, Savings and Debts in a Changing World: Developing Sociological and Anthropological Perspectives, 14–16 May 2001, Wageningen, the Netherlands.
2 See Roland Littlewood and Goffredo Bartocci, 'Religious Stigmata, Magnetic Fluids and Conversion Hysteria: One Survival of "Vital Force" Theories in Scientific Medicine?', *Transcultural Psychiatry* 42, 2005, pp. 596–609; and Daniel M.T. Fessler, 'Starvation, Serotonin, and Symbolism: A Psychobiocultural Perspective on Stigmata', *Mind and Society* 6 (3), 2002, pp. 81–96.
3 I am very grateful to Brian Watermeyer for helping me think through these ideas. See also Brian Watermeyer and Leslie Swartz, 'Conceptualising the Psycho-Emotional Aspects of Disability and Impairment: The Distortion of Personal and Psychic Boundaries', *Disability in Society* 23, 2008, pp. 599–610.
4 See http://www.nlm.nih.gov/medlineplus/ency/article/001228.htm.

5 Interview with Mark Raphael Baker, http://www.harpercollins.com.
au/author/AuthorExtra.aspx?displayType=interview&authorID=
50000641.

CHAPTER 7

1 See http://www.thedreambuildersinc.com/media/MikeE-kit.pdf.

2 See Kathleen McDougall, "'Ag Shame" and Superheroes: Stereotype
and the Signification of Disability', in Brian Watermeyer, Leslie
Swartz, Theresa Lorenzo, Marguerite Schneider and Mark Priestley
(eds), *Disability and Social Change: A South African Agenda*
(Cape Town: HSRC Press, 2006), pp. 387–400; and Kathleen
McDougall, Leslie Swartz and Amelia van der Merwe (text for work
with photographs by Angela Buckland), *Zip Zip My Brain Harts*
(Cape Town: HSRC Press, 2006).

3 Sandra M. Gilbert and Susan Gubar, *The Madwoman in the Attic:
The Woman Writer and the Nineteenth-Century Literary Imagination*,
2nd ed. (New Haven, CT: Yale University Press, 2000), p. ix.

4 http://www.idahostatesman.com/110/story/476785.html.

5 Erik Weihenmayer, *Touch the Top of the World: A Blind Man's Journey
to Climb Farther than the Eye Can See: My Story* (New York: Plume
Publishers, 2002).

6 http://wcbstv.com/sports/miss.usa.cerebralpalsy.2.697090.html.

7 Greg Walloch, 'Fuck the Disabled', in Bob Guter and John R.
Killacky (eds), *Queer Crips: Disabled Gay Men and Their Stories*
(New York: Haworth Press, 2003), pp. 4–5.

CHAPTER 8

1 For a more complete description, see Kathleen McDougall, Leslie
Swartz and Amelia van der Merwe (text for work with photographs by
Angela Buckland), *Zip Zip My Brain Harts* (Cape Town: HSRC Press,
2006), pp. 78–79.

2 'One-armed presenter is scaring children, parents tell BBC', *Daily
Mail Online*, 23 February 2009, http://www.dailymail.co.uk/news/
article-1152466/One-armed-presenter-scaring-children-parents-tell-
BBC.html.

CHAPTER 9

1 For two insightful novels about this period, see Pat Barker, *Regeneration* (New York: Viking, 1991); and Sebastian Faulks, *Human Traces* (London: Hutchinson, 2005).

2 See Isabel Menzies Lyth, *The Dynamics of the Social: Selected Essays* (London: Free Association Books, 1990); and Isabel Menzies Lyth, *Containing Anxiety in Institutions: Selected Essays* (London: Free Association Books, 1992).

CHAPTER 10

1 Tom Shakespeare, *Disability Rights and Wrongs* (London: Routledge, 2006), p. 11.

2 David Leavitt, *The Indian Clerk* (London: Bloomsbury, 2007), p. 69.

CHAPTER 11

1 http://www.southtravels.com/africa/zimbabwe/crestacchurchillhotel/# description.

2 I discuss this in 'Building Disability Research Capacity in Low-Income Contexts: Possibilities and Challenges', in Malcolm MacLachlan and Leslie Swartz (eds), *Disability and International Development: Towards Inclusive Global Health* (New York: Springer, 2009), pp. 91–103. This paragraph is a slightly modified version of a paragraph in that chapter.

3 Valerie Sinason, *Mental Handicap and the Human Condition: New Approaches from the Tavistock* (London: Free Association Press, 1993).

4 The term 'handicap' is for various reasons out of favour in disability studies at present but was not out of favour when Sinason wrote her book, and I keep using her terms as she wrote them.

5 Gubela Mji, Siphokazi Gcaza, Natalie Melling-Williams and Malcolm MacLachlan, 'Networking in Disability for Development: Introducing the African Network for Evidence-to-Action on Disability (Afri-NEAD)', in Malcolm MacLachlan and Leslie Swartz (eds), *Disability and International Development: Towards Inclusive Global Health* (New York: Springer, 2009), pp. 69–89.

6 See, for example, Jean Lave and Etienne Wenger, *Situated Learning:*

Legitimate Peripheral Participation (Cambridge: Cambridge University Press, 1991); and Etienne Wenger, *Communities of Practice: Learning, Meaning, and Identity* (Cambridge: Cambridge University Press, 1998).

CHAPTER 12
1 Brian Watermeyer, Leslie Swartz, Theresa Lorenzo, Marguerite Schneider and Mark Priestley (eds), *Disability and Social Change: A South African Agenda* (Cape Town: HSRC Press, 2006).

Do you have any comments, suggestions or
feedback about this book or any other Zebra Press titles?
Contact us at **talkback@zebrapress.co.za**